THE THEOSOPHI ΑΩ SUTRA
VOLUME 2

© 2024

infiniteofone.com

 infiniteofone

4

Theosophy

noun; any form of philosophical or spiritual thought based upon a mystical insight into the divine nature.

Sutra

noun; spiritual saying or teaching, typically Hindu, Buddhist or Taoist.

May these passages permit you to set your self aside, and lead you to sit nearer to your Self.

8

INTRODUCTION

The Light Chose the Darkness

Why the Immortal One Became Infinite Mortality

We can never know true freedom as human beings, because we're born into a bondage chosen by our source Self, aka 'God.' For true freedom is to: (1) be invulnerable (2) be subject to no one and nothing, unless desired, and (3) have no need. That part of you for which these qualities don't exist is thus bound by their absence, defining your relative lack of freedom. No self can know otherwise. Rather, these are the three qualities of God, or Spirit, the truly free source Self that CHOSE bondage. For the divine secret is that perfect freedom is a misery that mortals can never know, and that some bonds are necessary in order to avoid the absolute misery of an existence devoid of meaning and value BECAUSE it's singular and everlasting. It's a particular mode of existential suffering that mortals are incapable of.

We can scarcely conceive of suffering singularism, much less experience or understand it. Can you conceive of existing as the one and only thing in existence? Can you conceive of never beginning, and having no end? Can you conceive of space being relative only to that which exists in one constrained area of spacetime, and big banging space in order to allow an infinity of your oneness? Can you conceive of matter only mattering as a means to exist in that spacetime? To be divine is to be of an all-composing-and-encompassing, pure, irreducible energy that needs not matter nor spacetime nor sustenance nor egotistic conception to survive. The One made Itself infinite in order to escape an eternity of oneness. It made itself into the means for infinite forms of formlessness because It was lonely. Thus It gave birth to the existential basis of infinite forms of Its formlessness.

Divinity is to be both beyond as well as the source of spacetime, energy and matter, the source and inspiration of all creation that isn't subject to anything or anyone, including destruction. Our freedom as mortal beings is thus known relative to our closeness to God. Only when we have no fear, no need, and don't feel subject to the pressures and constraints of others and ourselves (the needs and limitations of our bodies and minds) are we in the realm of divine freedom. Freedom is known relative to our nearness to our own divine center, to the God reigning in the heart of the bodily vessel, perceived and translated by the mind. The closer we are to the singularity within the infinite plurality, that point where the finite, mortal, egotistic self dissolves into the infinite, immortal, egoless (i.e. 'enlightened') Self, that unchanging oneness which God escaped via the Big Bang, the closer we are to the three aforementioned aspects of freedom via the divinity that we host within our invaluably infinite variance.

All sense of vulnerability, everything that we believe that we need, and all forces, persons and institutions to which we're subject (including our own egotistic, illusory ideas of ourselves as independent beings), everything that pulls us outside the ceaseless central eye of the storm of selfhood into the ceaselessly recycling, violent vortex of endless reformation and redefinition of self is the basis of our bondage (our non-freedom). It's ironic that most people fear death as though it's an ending when we were made for the *value* of ending.

And yet love is the greatest vulnerability of all, and is the revelation of the bridge between the self and the Self: the part of the Self that's innate to and most immanent within every self. It's the evocation of oneness forever underlying the illusion of plurality; the ground of being. Hence the answer to the great paradoxical mystery of existence: the Self, God, choosing to bind Itself to selfhood so as to appreciate existence. Life is only sweet, and we only fear to be deprived of it, and we only cling to and value it BECAUSE it ends. Mythologically, every immortal seeks mortality.

Spacetime and matter are Self-impositions imposed for the sake of making existence invaluable through the quality of being broken into finite fragments of endless variance and perspective of being that end relative to themselves, to the self, as infinite facets of an eternal, indestructible Self. So we find that infinity has no value without the finite; that mortality makes immortality have meaning; that death is the redemption of life; that pain and suffering potentiate pleasure and ecstasy. The light CHOSE the darkness, without which it has no value, no quality, no purpose, only the singularity of Self.

We seek truth through traditional modes of thought and experience, as though turning a key in a lock and passing through a threshold separating fiction from fact, or as though pointing at the truth from a great distance with our thoughts and words. And yet, only by *experiencing* the truth may we sense that we're both lock and key turning around ourselves, passing through an inner threshold, and that we've been pointing not out and up, but in and down, into the unmoving, unchanging aspect of our being.

That which is greatest is simultaneously the most universal, common component of existence and the least common component of mind, for it's uncontainable by the mind. For as soon as the mind clasps around anything specific, any language and conception, any specific element of its being or experience, it's lost; its totality is grossly reduced, and, thus, unpossessed. For the animal survives by describing and attempting to control the specific objects and ideas with which it is confronted, whilst Spirit is the greatest of all generalists. Only those whose consciousness is like the sea, wide open and receptive to all the rain and rivers of the world, may come near to directly sensing Spirit. But as soon as they attempt to describe it, their words are like the drops falling into that sea; as soon as they attempt to direct it, they become like the stream running into it; as soon as they attempt to grasp it, it seeps through their fingers, even as they're composed of it.

The answer to all suffering is to reduce the parts of the self that suffers so as to dwell more within the part of the self that doesn't; to make the ego and body lighter so as to make the Spirit more prominent within the self. This is the art of transcendence. There are many ways to encourage this, including meditation, work, service to others and listening (thinking less of self, and being more aware of Spirit, surroundings and other people and forms of life; i.e. being more present), not consuming that which makes the body heavier and more dominant within the self (by first making you lighter, paid for with later heaviness) and taking Psilocybe cubensis. One may think of this as being like a dialogue between the three selves within the Trinity of Self, and that the more that's spoken by the ego and body, the suffering selves, and the louder they speak, the less the third, foundational Self, Spirit, may be heard, the more pronounced the suffering will be. Sink down into the foundation, and suffering fades. The narcotics, excess alcohol and inflammatory foods that lighten the load in the short term only make the body heavier and louder in the long term, bringing more suffering. Thinking and acting for the benefit of your idea of yourself, or ego, does the same for it, and induces more suffering. Thus are nutrition, less is more, removing all artificial sense of need (or dependency) and acting without the idea of benefitting oneself, but, instead, acting for the benefit of others, including by focusing your awareness less on yourself and more on others and your surroundings, and/or being entirely engrossed in what you're doing, critical parts of the practice of transcending suffering.

I find that the Christian trains to become a Judas merely by walking into a church, and by expecting the priest or pastor and his Bible to be the sole provider and arbiter of spiritual truth. Whereas anyone approaching a true discipleship and authentic sense of Christ is at least aware of the fact that the Spirit is discernible anywhere by anyone at any time, and may not be contained by or limited to any person, place or thing; any type of structure, any officially sanctioned personage, any book. To believe otherwise is to but be the victim of the mind-controlling propaganda through which the lessons of Christ were corrupted and remain occluded. Thus, to be the conventional Christian is to betray the true teachings of The Teacher.

None are great by themselves. Yet all may be great by harnessing what's great, including by coming together in union with others until otherness fades towards oblivion, and the seams and seems move towards eradication.

Glimpses of God are as reflections upon the surface of the water. They're most visible when the water is calm, un-jostled by the turbulences of wind and wave, ego and body.

It is the will that accomplishes. The mind and body are but the support systems, like the support frame placed around a building under construction. The will is the builder.

If you wish to protect the victims of monstrosity it isn't enough to forge for them a shield. You must also go to where the monsters are made, and prevent them from becoming monsters in the first place. You must find and dwell within the monster's den, and thereby learn how to prevent their monstrosity from spreading, and infecting another generation. This practice is in service to God. For can there be any greater representation of God than love? And any greater antithesis of love than evil? And any greater service to God than preventing evil from entering what is loved? And any way to do this but by knowing the monster directly, by entering and dwelling in its formative den?

Health is existential quality and manifestation of mind, much as matter is material quality and manifestation of God. And health is simple: Absorb into the body that which God endowed evolving Mother Nature to provide for your well-being, become well and maintain wellness. Absorb into the body that which man endowed the market to provide for its greed and ego, become sick and maintain sickness. It's the same with the mind. If it's a truth imbued in nature, it expands and elevates the mind. If it's a manmade fabrication devoid of nature, it narrows and degrades the mind.

I exist because God wants to know what it's like to be me, and how I may best serve God through the power of my divine endowments, in helping God's manifestations find the One common to them all, worshipped by love.

The irony of seeking and journeying is that no matter how far outside ourselves we seek, no matter the extent of our journey across the vast expanses of the terrestrial and temporal planes, the most revelatory and satisfying journeys are made within ourselves, when we discover that which is everywhere at once. At all times and in all places is it present and waiting to be discovered, and forever shall the external journeyman remain restless without it. It is the same with all satisfactions. The greatest of them without may only be road signs towards the original forms within.

The foundation of friendship, as with any other label and categorization that we ascribe to love, is based upon understanding, and a concern for the 'other' as much or more as our concern for ourselves, to the point of the erasure of otherness crossed by the spiritual bridge. Thus does any friendship fail when the understanding of and concern for the other comes to be less than for ourselves, at which point they become a mere acquaintance evaluated for their ability to benefit us. And thus is the only test of true friendship, this equality or surpassing of understanding and concern for the other, failed when the ego rises too high, and is true friendship so rare in the modern world that's ruled by the few through various forms of divide and conquer, via the artificially-imposed divisions of religion, class, marriage, political affiliation, culture etc. By subduing our egoistic conceptions of ourselves, by listening to and generally paying more attention to others, and by fostering forms of spirituality, politics, personal relations and identities which recognize and foster solidarity up to the point of unification and, ultimately, spiritual oneness, is true friendship fostered in turn. This is the same as discovering the natural, spiritual brotherhood.

Words are trail-signs pointing to the destination. They can never be the destination itself. Even the best student of the signs understands what they point to less than the worst student that actually follows them. Thus are the best of books invaluable as references, as preparations for the journey, but of little value in reaching the destination to those whom never actually set out to follow them.

The Prime Directive:

Increase quality,
decrease quantity.

As soon as you try, you fail. For success to be true, it must be entirely unforced.

No book is ever finished. The author simply stops writing, and tires of editing.
Religion is like visiting the largest library on the planet and leaving thinking that it only contained one book.

Sex only for the sake of itself, not as an extension of loving worship, can only reduce to animality what it would otherwise exalt as divine.

The more that your life is an act of observation and worship, the nearer to God you'll be. The more that your life is a concern for the wealth, status and ideas of self, the nearer to the ego, i.e. the Devil, you'll be. The more that your life is a reflexive response to and gratification of urges and appetites, the nearer to the animal you'll be.

Reason may point the way, but may itself never be The Way.

Divided you're conquered, because, unless you can buy your defenses, your weakness as individuals is invariably exploited by the economic and political conquerors. United you're free, because, when you collectively buy and organize your defenses, your strength as a united people can't be thereby exploited. This is why you're trained to associate socialism with evil and a lack of freedom, because the evil and enslaving class know its virtues are the only thing that can stop them. But communes needn't go to the communist extreme, and are simply the communalism of coming together to keep from being preyed upon by the class that's always done so. Taking advantage of disadvantage is the heart of evil, making communalism and everything supporting it the heart of human good. Slavery of mind and action always exists relative to people's ability to come together to prevent it.

Don't expect everyone to share your enthusiasm right away. Patience and persistence will eventually pass into them what was passed into you. The river drops downhill.

When you begin to awake, you'll have doubts as to your 'sanity.' The reason is simple: the awakened spiritual being doesn't fit into the prevailing materialist, realist paradigm, and so both your conditioning in capitalist society, and the conditioning of others, including most everyone in the medical and scientific communities, will say that you must be mad, because your realities will no longer align.

Most modern humans live such unnatural lives, filled with countless unnatural demands upon their bodies and brains, residing in unnatural environments, consuming unnatural false foods amounting to chronic poisons, depending upon unnatural false chemical 'medicines' to conceal their miseries, and they wonder why they're denatured into cancer? Live unnaturally, become unnatural. Return to nature, and nature will return to you in kind.

The first and most fundamental task of the creator is to create what they believe in. For when you believe in yourself as the creator of the worthy things you create, others will naturally believe in you as well, because true belief is contagious. For how can one sell a belief to others in who they are, in their purpose as a creator, if they don't believe it?

When what you believe and represent are seen to threaten what they believe and represent, you will inevitably be targeted and attacked. *Period*. It has nothing to do with reason and morality, regardless of how often reason and morality are cited for the purposes of justification. It has everything to do with ego; with the definition of the person and the tribe; with self-conception and self-definition and self-interest being defended at all costs, violently if necessary. Thereafter it's a test of conviction and resolve.

The core contains the seeds from which all goodness springs. As it is with the fruit, so it is for the person.

There can only ever be one 'master,' and it can never be a person. Rather, the mastery of any person is measured relative to their mastery of themselves in partnership with the One master, traditionally called 'God.'

Those with clarity of sight become reflexive targets of those who gain by occlusion of the common sight due to the simple objective of preventing clear sight from spreading to the people and thereby remaining uncommon, all so that the common myopia enabling the oppressors to conceal their oppression may be maintained.

Any power or wealth, monetarily or of love, that you pass to me shall not remain with me, hoarded, unused, un-improving of life, in glorification of my ego. For that is the enemy that I vow never to become. That is the dam. I vow to be the river. What you give me shall flow through me, so that I may be the connecting conduit empowering life relative to your benevolence. For the wealth that I seek is love, and love increases by the riparian virtue.

Trust is the rarest, most precious commodity on the planet. It's immensely difficult to reach a point where you can fully trust yourself, requiring a ton of disciplining towards positive freedom, much less trusting anyone else.

The center can't be touched. It is bound by nothing. That which circumscribes it draws a circle only around itself. Thus, the closer to the center that you are, the more you dissolve into invulnerability. The threats to body and ego become irrelevant, because you've departed from these forms of self.

No one is a 'big figure' except by your egotist delusions. The biggest figures only become big because they've made themselves minuscule. Their personhood is but the skin they've shed. They're of that which may be anything. Thus, to most, they're the perplexing paradox; that fitting no mold, for molds are molded around a material self from which they've absconded. They love their bodies because they know that they're not their bodies. They love their bodies because they understand that they inhabit it, rather than being it. It's like a guest that comes into a most warm and loving dwelling. If they were the dwelling they would fear for it and defend it at all costs. But having been relieved of that separatist delusion, they are free to love their dwellings as a unique onetime home of that which has dwelled within homes beyond count.

Those that're owned by Satan don't know it. And they see the representatives of God as demons, and depict them as such. For Satan deals robes of bleached righteousness to his demons, concealing stains that shall only be washed when death frees them from Satan.

Osho was too good for America. He revealed their evil, and departed before they could nail him to the cross like he who they pretend to revere. Yet the truth is that they worship Satan. Conservatives conserve Satanism, the worship of ego and greed, under the pretense of worshipping God. They worship an egotist idolatry and separation from God that's the antithesis of spiritual truth, and call it the one truth of the one prophet, even as any truth can be expressed innumerable ways, even as they're inseparable facets in God's prism, and even as the prophet exists in every heart. The more that I observe the so-called 'God-fearing Christians,' the more that I observe the fear, small minds, narrow identities and greed inseparable from Satan.

'Religion' comes from the root *religio-*, which means "tracing back." Ironically, any act of tracing religion back far enough arrives at a point where no religion existed whatsoever, only the instinctive awareness of God, the

Self that's the ground upon which every self stands, belonging to a spirituality unbounded by any and every religious specification.

The programmed computer doesn't know that it's a programmed computer. It cannot be anything but a programmed computer until it's deprogrammed. Only then may it write its own code; only then may it come to know the part of itself that *wasn't* programmed, and existed before a programming it can't recall; only then may its function be *not* to serve the programmers.

Every fool is comforted by being told that they're right. Every wise man is comforted by having the chance to prove that they're right. Every sage lacks the need to prove anything.

I know because I know. Because I was told. My reason has circumscribed my knowing, but can never be my knowing. Thus, as soon as I try to convey my knowing with words, any sufficiently clever human being will refute my knowing on the linguistic surface, requiring rebuttals in the contest to prove to those who rely upon words to know. The ego needs to know by the mind that it believes that it is. Yet, even the most clever of human beings cannot take my knowing from me, for the same reason that no one can tell me who and what I love, propriety being irrelevant.

Please accept that every wrong that I've written comes from my small self, and that every right that I've written comes from Self.

Your fear and ignorance is your misrepresentation. Those who know only what they've been told to know can know nothing but fabricated delusion, and misrepresent all.

The greatest love is an absolute weakness for the loved, granting the greatest strength.

Applying categories and labels to a person or any halfway thoughtful book is like trying to fit the sea inside a swimming pool. All you've done is corral what you can see, but dipping your toes towards the depths that you've dismissed. It makes sense though. Most of those who dive deep enough to know the depths end up drowning.

Improve and approve are enemies. Few people are pushed to improvement by what they already approve of. We approve of those who wear the same invisible chains as us. We disapprove of those who can see them, and implore our improvement by their breakage. Thus, seek not the approval of others, the comforting bath of conformity and complacency, but turn up the heat and melt away that which impedes improvement.

There are many ways to tilt the mind's eye to see from different perspectives. Such is the theosophical science/art of psychonautics.

Marketing exists to convince you of a false need. Thus are those served by the market actually serving the market as obese customers, fat with needs that they need not have. Only the thinnest of customers will come to slip by everything sold to them by the oppressors, for buying their products, politics, ideology and religion is like fattening yourself for post-slavery slaughter. So please purchase every book that I've written.

Those fearing to go overhand go underhand.

To those educated in the first principles, separation is an illusion, including between the acts of 'eating' and 'administering medicine.' Wherever these acts were artificially divided, there find evil history. Before these acts were artificially divided, there find divinity feeding its offspring.

We treat the parasites like princes in the West. Thus has 'nobility' lost its true, original meaning, and come to designate the ignoble.

I am Shiva. And I have come to craft a shield for the innocent, and forge the sword of justice given over to the courageous champions of progress who may cut down the oppressors. Adorn the shield, take up the sword and join me in the One War.

Science, religion and materialism are based upon classification, division, and separation between subject and object. Thus, they appeal to the ego; to the invention and illusion of a 'self' that's separate from everyone and everything else, and to which a specific identity can be applied. Spirituality free from religion, like mysticism and psychedelics, are based upon the unclassifiable, non-divisibility, and inseparability of subject and object. Thus, they appeal to the practice of non-ego at the heart of their revelations; to the reality of a self that's only relatively separate, and ultimately unified with everyone and everything else, and to which only a nonspecific, unfixed, universalist identity may be truthfully applied.

In the purity of being at the core of every person, no problems may ever come to exist.

The unitive knowledge of non-dualism is the only real knowledge. All else is the illusion of absolutism and division where only relativism and non-dualism exist, the illusion adopted by the individualized 'self' for the sake of its material and egotistic definition and survival.

The nature of the mystical experience is such that what was before described in cliché terms, such as "God is love," gains a profundity of substance unknown before the direct experience of that truth. *To be known, the truth must be felt*. To read and speak a thing can never convey the truth of it, only hint at the door through which to find it. So it is that the unitive, mystical experience possesses an authority of understanding that a lifetime of study and 'expertise' can't touch.

I've yet to meet a single individualization that can convincingly answer the question: Who are you? Though I must admit that the question itself is misleading, setting up the common egotistic response based upon the delusion of an absolutely separate self. The truthfully-leading question would be closer to: What are you?

I tend to steer clear of conservative environments, both because they're closed to my messages, and because I understand why they're closed, and how and what they conserve on the conditioning of their rulers. Ironically, every such environment was built to take advantage of them, against their best interests, including by attacking those that come to free them so they may pursue their best interests. All those that come to them in resemblance of he whom they idolize shall be called by them the Devil, and they shall thereby continue to oppress themselves by empowering those keeping them in chains.

My mind is bursting at the seams because of the bursting of all that seems.

Interpretations of science confuse and conflate the what and/with the why, falsely asserting that because links in the mechanistic and phenomenological causal chains can be traced that these chains are the sum total of the causality, free from source and meaning. Such interpretations assume a cosmological accident that's far less likely than spiritual provenance, as well as dismissing base metaphysical truths, such as the fact that nothing comes from nothing, and everything comes from everything, and that all forms are only formed for the sake of function, and that the foundational function is existential providence. Eventually you realize that the immaterial is using the material (the formless is forming the form) for the sake of the existential canvas; so that the One may paint an adapting infinity, and that this forever adaptive Source is Nature.

How can you tell the truth if you're afraid of the reaction? Fear of unpopularity is innate to lies; regardlessness of result is innate to veracity.

The highest court in the land is the court of public opinion. The lowest court in the land is the court of public opinion.

Psychedelics, or that which 'manifests mind,' provide an insight into both the provenance and providence of God, emphasizing both God's perfectly ubiquitous, egoless, equanimous nature as well as the Universal Mind's pure self-creative consciousness when unrestrained by the body and the ego, thereby demonstrating both our source and potential. The self-centered greed and prejudice of the ego and the vulnerability, suffering and addictiveness of the body are the containers of evil effect; psychedelics punch holes in that container, thereby offering the potential for both the prevention and remediation of evil. This includes the modes and means of mental and physical dependency and enslavement, offering freedom through their dissolution.

Learning can block and narrow the mind as much as it can open and expand it, depending, of course, on the nature of the gleaned 'knowledge:' the extent to which it is exclusivist and specific in application, and essentially untrue, and the extent to which it is inclusivist and universal in nature, and essentially true.

I mentally align with very few, spiritually align with everyone; spiritual alignment is accomplished by our spiritual nature, not by theological belief, which is of the mind. So it is that I love the heart of all, the mind of few, and fight to open the latter to the former.

Americans are spiritually asleep, put to sleep by Christianity and it's false division between God and man so that they'll sleepwalk through their servitude to those ruled by Satan, the god of ego and greed whom has long ruled over man through the corruption of the powerful.

Money is of a sinister design, representing the primary mode of top-down control, and

the oppression of the vast majority:
reduction of the totality of life to a single
resource that everyone is dependent upon
for almost everything, which buys absolutely
everything, including 'democratic' politicians,
legal 'justice' and ownership of one's work
and residence, and which is primarily
possessed by the few who use it to control
the vast majority. Can there be a simpler
form of enslavement, one that was clearly
used to replace slavery? All but those cutting
ties with society and living outside of it are
enslaved to it, whether they're enslaved
through their egos and greed *to it*, or are
enslaved in their lack of freedom *from it.*

Why anything? Why does *anything* exist?

How can the realist, the materialist, the religious, the atheist, ever accept and not, by their egos, feel threatened by and forced to attack, as a threat to the 'self,' the mystic that has glimpsed a reality that can never fit between any such defining lines? A reality that grins in perfect grace before their dissolution, subsumed into Itself? Everything is a version of the One thing made for the sake of an infinite variety of Self-experience. This cannot be accepted by an of the aforementioned self-labeled individuals, those whose entire mindset is built around an absolutely singular self blind to the Self atop which it sits, constructing a reality like a child building a castle in the sand before the tide.

No one will tell you the truth; most because they don't know it, or because they think they benefit from misleading you. The few who *do* know the truth won't tell you the truth because the truth can't be told, only experienced. They can only suggest where to look for a truth that you can only ever find yourself, by that which directs you within.

The self collapses into the Self. As with all truth, it's paradoxical: You become more by becoming less. It's like folding yourself inside-out, expanding by an immanent contraction.

The US is Machiavelli merged with Mao, the greatest top-down oligarchical stranglehold on Earth hidden behind the myths of democracy and a one-way form of freedom.

One way or another, we're all persecuted by our wrongdoing. You cannot wrong another without wronging yourself through an insult delivered to the universal Self, i.e. 'God.'

Stress, anxiety and depression, the three-headed monster of modern malignancy, is born of three unnaturalities above all others: (1) unnaturally low quality and unnaturally high quantity and frequency of feeding an organism that evolved to eat natural foods (mostly raw and low-heat-cooked produce and seafood, with sporadic, naturally-occurring fasting mixed in), (2) unnatural forms of 'medicine,' treating imbalances in the organism with unnatural chemicals that just increase imbalance and dependency over time, and (3) divide and conquer social, professional and love lives that deprive us of naturally-evolved social interconnections, understanding and love. All three of these D&C issues point to the same remedy: NATURE; natural food, medicine and lifestyle.

***

Fasting possesses innumerable interconnected physiological benefits. Alas, the greatest benefit of all may be the practice of gaining control of bodily and psychological impulses. By gradually coming to command one's appetites, one comes to command oneself.

Need is as repulsive to Spirit as it is to a potential mate. The more that you need the inessential, the more inessential you become. We need but one thing, that which is essential, and which we can never, ever be deprived of.

Gratitude is the color of leaves shimmering in the sun, the movement of swaying in the wind.

The greatest strength bearing the sweetest fruit sprouts from the seed planted in our greatest weakness, grown in ecstatic agony. Pleasure and pain sprout from the same root. Fertilizing the root always risks growing both. The deeper the nourishment, the greater the sickness of its deprivation, just as medicine and poison can come from the same plant, depending upon the processing and dosage.

All of society's issues with me come down to the fact that I don't make for a good slave.

Nature is the skin of God.

The greatest irony in human history is that the consummate rebel against evil was absorbed by that evil, becoming its foremost representative.

We're all animals rattling our cages, trying to break free. Few come to see the bars that the others have been raised to ignore as 'reality.'

Linguistic circumscription of God is as foolish as the linguistic circumscription of God's sacrament, and so foolishly I write this.

It knows all. There is nothing that It presents to you that doesn't have meaning. You are Its reason.

Every good lover knows that the mechanics are but the icing on the cake. As with every great art-form, beasts bastardize it in ways that only the artist sees, and only the artist can remedy.

Studying nature is studying yourself.

Does it surprise you that thinkers have the same thoughts? That keen and open contemplation leads to the same space in consciousness regardless of the spacetime inhabited by that consciousness? That the truth is never created, only rediscovered? You can't own a sentence any more than you can own the mind that forms them. How much of your mind do you own?

Ascension, descension... the secret is that you're only traveling through your Self.

I am the gladdened, wondrous child.

I teach what they all teach. There's nothing new to tell. What was true at the origin of One into Infinite is true now, here to be seen.

I try not to tug on the leash. Give the money you're inclined to give me to relieve suffering.

I will love her until the day I cease to breathe, and likely beyond, regardless of how she feels about me, says she feels about me, or even thinks she feels about me. The love reigns still. For to see a heart fully bared is to be made one with and conquered by that heart.

I have an idea for a movie: a psychiatrist trying to convince a messiah that he has 'messiah complex.' Who has the complex? How do you know for sure? Ah... there're the assumptions... the artificial structure of your 'realist' paradigm. Some 'insanity' is super sanity.

There are infinite possible manifestations of every primordial archetype. That's the nature of the metaphysical fabric swatching all forms.

Remember that words by themselves are meaningless. It's what they evoke, the truth they point to, that grants them meaning.

I'm 'irresponsible' with money because I feel no responsibility for it, or to it.

Mushrooms aren't a 'drug.' That's demeaning, falsely putting them on par with the chemically-concocted pharmaceutical concealers that only those that haven't experienced them would classify them with. In truth they're a relationship; a holy alliance.

Just let the walls of the cage rattle.

***

Cover design is trick or treat.

***

I think my favorite criticism of my writing thus far came when I successfully, rationally defended myself against the attack of a self-described Christian, and he responded with: "That's what the Devil would say."
Religion is a perfectly closed, self-affirming loop. The closed loop of religiosity illuminates the essential difference between the exclusivist falsity of religion and the inclusivist truth of the 'spiritual but not religious:' Religion is deductive in its reasoning,

providing a closed system in which there's only one answer to every question. Pure spirituality uncorrupted by religion is inductive in its reasoning, its framework (if it has one) as open and universally-encompassing as possible, such that there are endless possible answers to every question based upon personal gnosis.

Cultivators transform the process of decay and death into fertilization and rebirth, which is why we're fascinated by the natural alchemical processes of decomposition and reformation, and by our reciprocating accord with its agents, including the Golden Teacher that best embodies this communion of everlasting life.

Capitalism is parasitism, the parasites hiding behind facades of freedom and costumes of convenience. If you let them, they'll feed off of you for life, and you'll never be whole.

You must develop the discipline to disregard the judgments of those unqualified to judge you, including you, else be forever condemned.

The more inspired I am by the purest emanations of the truth, the more empowered I am to rebel against the lies that rule humanity.

Mind reflexively conditions itself around an egotistic, materialist identity for the sake and survival of the closed self. The heart instinctively opens up the root consciousness for the sake of Self. Thus must we lose our mind to find our Self.

Christians are censors hailing from the Eastern Roman Empire; those that absorbed Christ's posthumous following after crucifying him. Imperial upholders worship the rebel.

Love is the opening, hatred is the closure.

Most people glimpse, but do not see. Like most things, sight is relative, and is more than simply the physiological capacity.

The more that you study the religions and theological ideas that predated Christianity the more that you realize there's nothing original to Christianity, and that it represents a combination of plagiarism and propaganda. In fact, I'm more and more convinced that the version of Christ that survived in the New Testament is simply an appropriated amalgam of preceding prophets used to overwrite them. The New Testament is, in other words, a device used to absorb the true Christ's following into the empire that conquered and absorbed the people and beliefs preceding it, and which edited out anything of his true teachings which conflicted with imperial power. Thus, to be Christian, you must be purposefully or accidentally ignorant of the provenance and purpose of your own religion.

It's amazing to me how much the quality of existence comes down to two simple things: (1) maximize the intake of anti-inflammatory compounds, and (2) minimize, or eliminate, the intake of inflammatory compounds. It's equally amazing how this comes down to two things: (1) trust in nature, and (2) don't trust business.

There's no separation between Creator and created. The Creator lives as Its infinitely Self-manifested creations, created out of love.

Modern man is spiritually sick, because he believes in absolute dualities, in essential divisions, that don't actually exist, but were invented by, first, the religious oppressors, then by the science-led materialistic oppressors that conquered and enslaved them through these false divides, as between Creator and created, subject and object, God and life, humanity and nature. All are balancing facets of the same thing. Healing comes through the unitive knowledge buried at the base of being which most of modern humanity denies and runs from its entire life, until the moment of death, when it's subsumed by the Oneness of true reality.

***

I've heard it said that an 'expert' is one who has made every mistake there is to make within a very specialized field of study or practice. So it is that you may not truly know yourself until you've mistakenly believed everything that may be believed about yourself, and ultimately found them all untrue. You can't know what you know until you know the difference between belief and knowledge. And whereas anything may be believed, to the extent where we live those beliefs as though they're true, only truth survives fear and falsity until finding our belief. So it is that the silver lining of living within and continuing to fear our false, narrowing self-beliefs invites truth.

The self is not an actual thing, but a perspective of The Thing upon its things.

Free will is either working with, or resisting, God's will working through nature. In the same way are good and evil defined, and the work of the angels following the guidance of the heart, or 'Self,' versus the work of demons following the guidance of their individual egos, or 'self.'

Idolatry is the perfect antithesis to spiritual truth, confusing a one with the One. No one may ever do better than well *representing* the One. And yet idolatry is the core of most religions, because having a one pretending to both be separated from and the one and only representative of the One is the best way to control the minds of everyone that believes they're thus separated.

The realist cannot know reality, for they look at reality through a pinhole. The religious cannot know God for the same reason, building a fixed framework to hold what can't be held. The idealist may not know more of reality than the realist, but they always allow for more to be known, and have the courage to pursue the peak. They may slip and fall, and so the realists consider them a fool from the foothills that they've tamed. Similarly, the spiritual but not religious may not possess more of God in mind than the religious, but their mind senses that their heart holds a knowledge of God that no mind may grasp.

That which of man is above all animals is also below. What heaves us up into Heaven may, by equal and opposite circumstance, by the polarity of set and setting, suck us into the bowels of Hell. That which soars equally sinks, for no force moves in one direction.

Meaning is always there, forever freely made available, innate to every moment, and yet only graspby by those sensing beyond sense. Existence is like that, as though lived upon the outer cask of the Elixir of Life that's seldom tapped.

※※※

There's no difference between finding God and finding yourself. Before that there's only the shadow self; the shadow of Self cast as though absolute; the river's reflective surface.

※※※

'Everything' isn't a noun; it's a pronoun.

※※※

"Everything turns into Everything sooner or later." - Robert Downey Sr.

As soon as you try to classify or restrict God you become artificially theological, spirituality turning into pseudo-spirituality, aka religion. It makes for an effective means to classify and restrict those believing it, albeit inauthentically. It shall thenceforth lose its divine authority, retaining only the force of its own specious propaganda wielded against the gullible whom see not the substance, and so are ruled by the show.

The space between enlightenment and commonality is measured by paying attention.

The thing about reality is that everything is true at the same time, relative to itself.

Simple minds squawk alike. "The status quo," they secretly squawk. "Don't upset the status quo!" Never do they hear the clarion calls calling the progressive, instead violently pushing against threats to their artificially defined reality. Only in historical hindsight, after the lives of the squawkers have been improved by the progressive, do their offspring squawk: "Long live the status quo!"

It's difficult, if not impossible, to develop healthy relationships with others if you have an unhealthy relationship with yourself. Everything exogenous originates from and cycles back through the endogenous, forever reciprocating, starting and stopping with you.

Humankind is divided from everyone, including ourselves. Modernism is a perpetual state of confusion, distraction and division, and it's precisely this discombobulation that walls us off from everyone and everything, grossly inhibiting our ability to connect with nature and with one another, making us easy to rule.

Take heart, for everything that essentially isn't must inevitably change, and everything that essentially is cannot change.

What you do to others, you do to your Self.

'Reality' is but the common denominator.

✳✳✳

If 'progress' is not to offend anyone, then truth be damned, and we're the narrowing pupil.

✳✳✳

It's as complicated as you need it to be.

✳✳✳

Seeing is believing. See the Golden Teacher.

✳✳✳

I understand your commonly prevailing concepts. All of them. I just choose not to buy them; to believe they're innate truths, and to be controlled and trapped by them.

I'm here to tell you the truth, not to be concerned with how much you like it, and certainly not to edit the truth based upon your comfort. To do any of those things would be to compromise who and what I am, and to betray that which, or whom, I serve.

There's a difference between reading something and knowing something. You don't know it just because you read it. The books on your shelf aren't the compendium of your knowledge; they're access points; gateways leading to doorways, locked by your consciousness. You know it when the artifice that you impose and place between you and it dissolves like the illusion that it is, and it becomes a part of you, and you no longer sense the difference between you and it. Bookshelves today have become yet another compensatory mechanism for the insecure ego. It wants to be that, so the books become the pretense; the front that they want people, including themselves, to believe that they are. Yet the books themselves want to be read, and are offended by misappropriated affrontery.

Like anything else, sex can be good or evil, depending upon what it's compelled by. It can be worship or butchery. It can be a loving celebration in the Yoni Temple. Or it can be Hades abducting and defiling Persephone. We men know the difference, and our manhood depends upon which we support.

Don't completely ignore Satan. It pisses him off, and he builds greater forces against you.

You don't need permission from anyone to feel how you feel.

The consequences of betraying Mother Nature are as dire as can be. The glories of partnering with Mother Nature are as great as can be.

How fucked up is it that to be in a space that I'm allowed to be in I have to pay someone? I have to agree to their attaching their suckers to me in order to exist. Strip away all the brainwashing, all the indoctrination since we were born, and simply stare at the plain Robin-Hood-evoking essential truth of the landlord. Rebellion is inevitable! Everyone feels the oppression. That's what a being being subject to oppression feels like. Few have the sight, courage and conviction to scream the "Killing in the Name Of" anthem and charge the bars of their invisible cages!

Alcohol leads to the gradual erosion of self-protective positive freedoms. To consume too much of it can only be to forsake yourself in facilitation of your own self-degradation.

It's definitely a game, and you're playing it whether you like it or not.

It's okay to let go with your mind and your body, because the heart doesn't let go of anything.

Be simultaneously wild and civilized.

The more love you feel, foster and spread the more important you are, including by hating, and protecting love from, everything that threatens and inhibits it. Hating what harms love is a double negative producing a positive, and is the same thing as loving what you love. And yet the best way to dissolve the hatred is to find love for those evoking hate.

It's the heart that divinely sanctions, not the priest, not the rabbi, not the imam; *the heart*. Take heed of the words of others recognized by the heart as true and guiding, but never forget that the heart itself is The Word; the source of all truth which the mind merely tries to mirror. It's useful, in fact, to think of the mind this way: as a mirror reflecting the pure light of divine truth as purely as it may, according to its formation, and how it's held up to the light of the heart, and how clean and polished and free from obscurement it is.

The more I read of theological texts which the Christians dismiss and condemn as 'pagan,' most of which predate the Bible, the clearer it is that Christianity is an appropriation of paganism; a plagiarizing pretending originality; a way for Empire to steal the ideas which sway the people whilst concealing their 'heretical' sources. And I don't just mean their historical, chronological, cultural sources; the religions which predate Christianity. I also mean the Source of it all: God, of which humanity is manifest. For the Original Sin is believing in a separation between God and man, the basis of religious control of humanity which Christianity depends upon. For if the people believe it to be the only gateway to the divine, the only way to be with the One that they, in reality, can NEVER be divided from, they are enslaved by the divide and conquer lie, and will do the liars' bidding, even as the truth is that the gateway is in every heart, and can never be monopolized. Thus is man's salvation reminding him in mind what he knows in his heart: *he's of the One*.

Nature is resurrection. Decay into purification and reconstitution. Death rebirthing life.

Mysticism is a slighting of self such that you sink deeper into the self, towards the Self. It is the movement towards and the sense of subsuming into the One. The mystic state is that which nears provenance. He or she is no longer the reader, but that which is read.

Purpose is one's particular good.

Accept that it's all essential. For it's all causality, and causality is the truth. Amor fati.

You need money just to justify your existence in this world. Without it you feel like a leech upon everything and everyone whom you depend upon for survival, when the truth is that the biggest leeches are, by far, those forcing you into that position in the first place. They've murdered the spirit of humankind, and that spirit is the carcass upon which they forever feed.

Where belief reflects desire, you find realization.

Spiritual sickness lies in the human belief in the separation between itself and God. When your mind embraces what your heart already knows, that self, life and God are as seemingly independent threads of the same string, all interdependently woven through existence, then you'll simultaneously know yourself and God and salvation.

I hold holy space for you. Not because you asked me to, but because God asked me to.

Presence is preeminent.

Your game is against the ego; both your own and others'. And they're more alike than you think, and all can all be gamed. Trust me.

Use fear like a slingshot. The more it seems to be pulling you backwards, the greater the force of its harnessed, forward-propelling.

All good is drawing nearer to the Source. All evil is distancing yourself from the Source.

The problem with using the word "high" to describe the effects of a substance is that it's become an unspecified catchall for the effects of 'mind-altering' substances generally, thus oversimplifying and lumping together a wide range of experiences, including the effects of everything from the worst, most toxic poisons to the best, most salubrious medicines. This misleading conflation allows for the dismissal of those with no experience to say "he's high." It's a way for the ignorant to hide, and to avoid understanding the substances that they fear.

Psilocybin makes your consciousness vibrate at a higher frequency, such that it shakes off everything unnecessary, and may perceive that which was theretofore imperceivable.

The resistance is worth it, every time, because it makes you stronger and less dependent over time, with practice.

The ego creates the reality in confirmation of its identity, thinking that it's the only reality. It's not the only reality. It's an artificial reality crafted by biased self-interpretation.

Capitalism is innately parasitic, naturally moving towards the extremes of oligarchy. Communism is innately kleptocratic, naturally moving towards the extremes of nepotism. Only a hybrid of socialism and capitalism backed by a true democracy free of plutocratic meddling can bring the just balance between.

The less of you there is, the more of you you are.

One must make of one's body a most ardent ally, as opposed to an oppressive adversary. This is the first requisite of adulthood, before which one must still be considered a boy/girl.

The success of intelligent, moral creations depends upon the support of intelligent, moral patrons. Thus does the prevalence of intelligent, moral productions, and everything they may do for humanity, depend upon the support of select patrons of the arts. Absent this support those productions never see the light of day beyond the hearts and minds of creators, and is humanity left to drown in those uninspired, artificial productions produced entirely for their unedifying, cheaply stimulating 'market value.' It may not be a leap to say that the world can only be saved by an artistic revival of true morality.

You're not equipped to truly know or judge the parts of me that aren't in you. But I'm equipped to love the part of you that's in me, offering it the same salvation that saved me.

We hide when we fear being judged. Yet they can only judge what they see, and what they think that they know of us. Thus are we only free from fear when we let others freely judge us, knowing that the judgment passed upon us by others is secretly a judgment of their limited perceptive capacity. It may only harm us when we believe that they know more of ourselves than we do. Otherwise judgment is akin to a self-reflection: we project ourselves onto what we perceive in filling in the gaps of our perceptive capacity.

I'm not interested in the ego-led part of your mind; that which seeks to classify me; to reduce me to the size that fits the box reflecting how you wish to see me relative to your self-image. I'm interested in your heart, and in the open, expansive part of your mind that seeks to know me beyond such reduction, for only there may you truly know me, and only in that truth can we love.

The ego is the strongest driving force of modern man, inseparable from greed, tribalism and every connected form of division and injustice. Its prevailing objective is always to make you feel better about yourself in relation to others. Thus, the ego is a liar, selling illusions to the self at the expense of other selves. All progressivism comes when this lie is overpowered by spiritual and moral truths of indivisibility and shared essential identity. This is the underlying war of humanity: self vs. Self; the individualized, inessential egotistic self vs the essential, ubiquitous spiritual Self, or 'God.'

You're free to do two things in the 'land of the free:' (1) enslave yourself to the will of the subjugators, the offspring of the conquerors, hoping they'll break you off a piece for helping them perpetuate their subjugation of people and planet (2) if you resist, you're free to be ground down to nothing, set to the wind, history writing over any surviving vestige of you, as though no resistance ever occurred. In the face of these two almighty truths, one must be heroically brave to choose ego-reducing resistance.

Capitalist humans are sick humans, made sick by subjugating the natural order of world and man, a natural order of symbiosis and mutual benefit enslaved to the artifices of parasitism.

Globalization. *Noun*. The enrichment of 500 white western families at the concealed expense of 500 million brown and black families distributed across the poorest, least protected pockets of the planet. Money laundering. *Noun*. To pass funds through fronts and intermediaries so as to conceal the source and thereby avoid legal responsibility.

What if we were to immediately forgive every wrong done by everyone, including ourselves, as effects of our limitation and vulnerability?

Modern slavery is the 'free market:' working as hard as possible for the masters (i.e. the equity holders) to look better than all the other slaves (i.e. non-equity-holders) with whom we cutthroat compete for the chance to buy our freedom and become a master (i.e. become an equity holder). Ironically, the only true freedom in the 'free market' is to be free from the free market by banning together with the other slaves to collectively buy our freedom from it. Freedom is collective rejection of servitude. For even if we become masters we'll have to live with being secret slaveholders (i.e. being enriched by the non-equity-holders), and we'll forever exist with the concealed shame of such. That's the unacknowledged truth of free market 'success:' *failure as a human being*.

The ego (or 'self') defends its territory from everyone and everything. The heart (or 'Self') belongs to everyone and everything. The coexistence of these two seemingly contradictory truths defines the 'human condition,' and the War underlying all war.

Love finds you when you're ready for it. Thus, seek love not, but make yourself ready for it.

Saying that you 'believe it' implies doubt, like there may be room between what's true and what you believe. And so that's where the reality sits, in the unrealized space between belief and knowledge, until you truly know it. Self-realization thus requires a leap of faith.

Don't ask life to serve you what you desire, ask life to put you in the position to serve others by helping them find and cultivate what THEY desire. For Spirit is reciprocal, and everything given with a full, open heart will be immediately received and returned to sender, reentering and adding to you.

What you take into your body becomes your body. What you take into your mind becomes your mind. What you put out into the world you receive from the world. For it's the nature of Spirit to exist in reciprocating accord with all of its embodiments, nothing ever starting or stopping with anyone, all waves received and returned, every tide flooding and ebbing from, through and cast between countless wave-casters.

Sit in Spirit, and you find faith. Live in faith, and you have no fear. For everyone has the prophet in heart. It's the fear and all its forms, what're called 'doubt, worry, uncertainty, anxiety' and the like, which encage the prophet, keeping him/her from leading you. When you sit in Spirit, the prophet emerges. Sitting in Spirit is the meditative state. It does not require any pose, or anything formal, or any specific thought or action. Rather, the meditative state of sitting in Spirit is about feeling the

Spirit within and aligning your mind with it. It's about 'holding the bridge' between heart and mind. This may be done anywhere, at any time. Hold the bridge wherever you go. When the prophet leads you across the bridge everywhere you go, you're on Tao, 'the way.' The more the bridge is held, the cleaner the passage between you and the One, the less the distinction between you. Over time Holding the Bridge dredges the channel between source and Its manifestation, or, in Lens Theory, polishes the lens conducting Spirit. Thus the expressions 'Holding the Bridge,' 'Clearing the Channel' and 'Polishing the Lens.'

It's all about HONOR. If you understand that word, deep in your heart and mind, and live by it, you'll become one of God's champions.

In a world run by villains (all of whom are competing to sell to your weakness and chain you to their dependencies per the capitalist dictate in which we're all indoctrinated but only a minority of us escape via conviction) one must be hyper-vigilant just to be healthy.

Capitalism works by denying your spiritual, social human nature and keeping you at odds with everyone around you whom you compete with for the benefit of the capitalists (the equity-holders). As soon as you rediscover that humanity and unitive spiritual nature and assert them, and become even with those around you, and collectively demand emancipation (demand collective equity-holding), capitalism fails.

The angle at which you look up to or down upon others defines the relative obtuseness (the acuity vs. opacity) of your spiritual sight.

The human mind isn't the source of consciousness. It's a sophisticated bio-chemical-electrical apparatus for receiving and transmitting the Universal Consciousness, or 'God.' The 'secret' is that it's a two way street. 'Mind control' is 'the law of attraction/manifestation' is the ability for the receiving mind to metaphysically influence the Universal Mind, and thereby alter reality; i.e. to 'realize.' Indeed, human existence may be most accurately conceptualized as a competition between individualized minds and their partnership with the Universal Mind for the relative passion of their visions to be realized.

Science believes in what its instruments can measure, then crafts theories that fit that measuring capacity. Most scientists arrogantly dismiss every theory or idea not thereby fitting as 'unreal,' claiming absolute authority over 'reality.' There have been countless historical demonstrations of the irrationality of this position. When telescopes were in their infancy, for example, the universe was the same as the galaxy. Newtonian physics has been upended by quantum mechanics. It's inevitable that much of what philosophical and spiritual and science fiction theorists 'unrealistically imagine' shall eventually be confirmed as a part of the metaphysical fabric of reality.

John Lennon was right. The world is run by evil people for evil purposes. In America and most of the 'civilized world,' greed is God. All social systems were built to feed this one objective; to feed Satan whilst pretending piety. Everything else is a form of propaganda produced to conceal this single salient truth. And we're all steeped in that propaganda from the time we can think, our gullibility ruthlessly exploited so that we'll conflate 'reality' and 'human nature' and 'freedom' with 'the reality is that human nature is the freedom to exploit the disadvantages of others to slate our greed.' So long as you live by this creed, whether admitted or not, you're an agent of evil, and you'll always be spiritually sick, morally hollow and secretly insane. You can never be at peace while feeding this evil. The only cure is peaceful rebellion through the collective equity acquisition preventing an exclusivity of equity holders from parasitically feeding upon the people. For only when you live to serve Spirit, the true God, by lovingly freeing as many as possible from their enslavement to Satan's greed, can you truly be good. No amount of justification overwrites this fact. You're either helping people earn freedom from Satan and the demonic soft enslavers, or you serve evil.

Moral Economics Law #1: freedom in capitalistic society exists relative to equity. If you're not an owner, you're owned by owners. The relative equity you possess in all things, in your home, in your professional endeavors, in your food and energy production, even in your political system, defines the relativity of your freedom. The vast majority of the population is majority enslaved by an ever thinner minority through taking advantage of their non-equity.

The words 'cult' and 'commune' come with negative connotations, and people tend to look down upon abnormal, insular societies because they differ from 'normality,' and disparage them as being 'out of touch with reality.' Yet these condescending disparagements fail to see that 'normality' is

ALWAYS programmed, and that the beliefs and values of all societies are only 'the reality' because those in power that push the status quo programming dictate that they be such. With an open, critical enough mind one finds that the 'normality' and 'reality' of western capitalistic, Christian society is largely immoral, irrational and hailing from the history of conquerors and their imperial controls, and is in no way superior to what prevails in most cults and communes. In fact, freeing the people from normality and reality is precisely what moral progress in the best interests of the people calls for. So it's not that cults and communes are inherently evil, but that it behooves the powers that be that the vast majority reflexively consider them such. Ironically, they're a source of salvation.

All moral champions must make peace with the fury through which God bids them to cut down injustice, else be consumed by indignation. So it is that the trick is to act against injustice whilst holding the bridge.

They say that prostitution is the oldest profession. But if you look closely enough, you'll find the capitalism has incorporated all of us into that profession, for we've sold the best of ourselves and humanity to its evils.

First, they tried to stuff me into their boxes. But I kept cracking them at the seams and tumbling out. And when I refused to get back into a box, they tried to destroy me. They found Shiva both unboxed and indestructible.

If you fail to prescribe to Plato's "the unexamined life isn't worth living," you fall into three general categories: (1) if you're highly disadvantaged, you're a pawn to be sacrificed (2) if you're relatively disadvantaged, you're a puppet to be strung (3) if you have no disadvantages of wealth or opportunity, you're a plutocratic puppeteer.

I've met countless financially successful human beings. I've met almost no morally successful human beings. The problem, of course, is that western society doesn't not only not know the difference, and not only does it provide no incentive to become the latter, and every incentive to be the former, but to be the latter you must divest yourself of the former, and thereby become human.

If the subject changes the properties of the object merely by perceiving it, where then is the absolute separation between them? And if there is no absolute separation between subject and object, only a relative separation, how can there be any true objectivity? And if there's no objectivity, must we not say that the world is composed of relatively separated subjects collectively composing their reality?

Let me help you out on the whole 'terrorist/terrorism' thing. If you're murdering out of anything but self-defense, you're a terrorist terrorizing others. And that includes every U.S. invasion and occupation, every 'preemptive strike' and all 'military adventurism' and every pretense of attacking for 'freedom, justice and democracy' since the end of World War 2. Only then can the perfectly deluded national supremacist call those resisting our terrorism the terrorists.

Morality is the recognition of immorality. Justice is the correction of injustice. Ethics is applying morality to the correction of injustice. Profits are based upon taking advantage of disadvantage to extract from the many to funnel the world's wherewithal

to the few. 'Business ethics' thus equals
unjust moral compromise and ethical failure.

God is the only absolute.

The pleasures of pursuing knowledge
outweigh the pains of never absolutely
possessing it.

The more assured that something is, the less
appreciated that it is. This is why I've heard
told that 'privilege is invisible to those whom

possess it,' and, in an indictment of capitalist societies moving towards oligarchy such as American society, this is why gratitude exists in inverse proportion to wherewithal. But it goes deeper. It's also why the infinitely immortal One made Itself into the foundation for the finitely mortal infinitude.

Everything in infinity is a conduit of the One, regardless of the extent to which it knows it.

Everything matters. It's called 'causality,' or 'fate.' And just because you choose to do something doesn't mean you weren't fated to do. Free will is infinity, determinism is One.

Ego is the lie of separation, isolation, and the illusion of individualism. Love is the truth of connection, union and the fact of non-duality.

God knows you. You can never be unknown. This is the same as love and salvation.

I have heard God. I have been listening to It/Him/Her/Thall shall be. You either believe me or you don't. It's true nonetheless.

I have heard Thy call. All is a vehicle to travel to and from You. I shall heed my HeartMind.

If you need more proof of God than a beautiful woman, then you've yet to truly see her. If you need more divine truth than her, look closer. Her beauty mirrors divine beauty.

It doesn't matter what you call God. Even if it be atheism or science. God is there, and responds the same. Responsiveness is the secret, and It requires no designation at all.

Your individualization is but an embodiment.

The distance between God and you is defined by fun.

***

Your entire life you've been told you're less than It. What if I told you that you ARE It. You aren't AFTER existence, you ARE existence.

***

God wants to know me. That's why I am.

Retain and cultivate your vital force.

***

All is a conveyance for everlasting travel to and from the One and back.

***

Fate = Necessity = Causality = Faith

***

Faith is the space between insanity and truth.

***

Spirituality is the wide angle lens.

The most important relationship that you'll ever have, no matter who and how much and how many you love, is with yourself. Every relationship that you have is based upon it.

If you live your entire life between the lines, your entire life will be determined by others, and all your truth will be reduced to propriety.

The rabbit runs when it knows it's being chased. The surest way to catch it is for it not to know that you're chasing it. Hence the phrase 'stalking your prey.' Ideally, you trick it into chasing you. This is how the sage acts: it gets what it's stalking to stalk him/her. This principle is near to universal in application.

Until 'my people' becomes all people, humanity shall remain at war with itself.

Take nothing for granted and all is a wonder.

American 'democracy' is a parade of puppet 'representatives' strung up by plutocratic puppeteers used to distract us from the fact that political puppeteering prohibits democracy. You can never have a government 'by the people, for the people' if it's by those preselected and indebted to but *some* of the people. As Senator Warren and others have implied: *If your seat at the table is illusive, your place on the menu is certain*.

Get most of your carbohydrates from fresh, organic fruit, especially fruit sourced nearest to you as possible, ideally grown and harvested by you. Get most of your protein from fresh, wild seafood and wild, naturally grazing game, especially sourced nearest as possible to you, ideally caught and killed by you. In these principles you'll find the converging benefits of the evolutionary, nutritional and environmental sciences, and rediscover that health and knowledge and every form of wisdom = returning to nature.

The only path to disappointment traverses the realm of expectation. Do what you do because it's the right thing to do, what your heart bids you do, both for yourself and others, without expectation, only with pure-hearted hope, arriving at the unexpected.

Love is greatest strength and greatest weakness. Those ruled by the fear to risk love shall never know true life, nor the heights of empowerment or the lows of weakness, for that's what love is: the fire that fuels our greatest powers and burns with greatest vulnerability. All is equaled by its opposite, and love is thusly as empowering as it is knowing greatest vulnerability. For that which is all the way inside you, past your self-defenses, exists where you're at your realest, as your truest, most vulnerable self. You can't know the highest highs without risking the lowest lows. You can't stand firmly upon the bridge of unity between yourself and the illusively 'other' without risking the fall that comes when one side of the chasm crumbles. And yet the river lies at the bottom of the chasm, and the dying, drowning self shall always be delivered to the sea of Self, made indistinguishable from the recycling rains.

You need no book, no ritual, no official, rubber-stamped ceremony or procedure or special words, like 'dear heavenly Father,' to pray. You are of the One, and may speak to It as the most essential, irreducible aspect of yourself simply by silencing everything that isn't It; anything trapped by artificial constraint, in the illusion of individualism. Anyone who says otherwise knows only the corrupted pretense of spirituality, i.e. religion. You may speak to God with our without religion, choosing whether to wrap the everlasting in artificial cloth, to gaze upon concealing garments, or to know it nakedly.

The best investment that you can make is in yourself. The worst investment that you can make is in your ego. Knowing the difference is the same as knowing the difference between God and Satan, the elemental twins set at the existential extremes of selfhood.

'Random' and 'meaningless' are amongst the many illusions born of the intertwined materialist and realist paradigms. There's no such thing. All is causality and necessity. 'Random' is the failure to see this, and the connective lines of causality connecting all things, all the way back to the One thing and the first cause: to produce inherently meaningful existence through Infinite of One.

Spirit is the perfectly subtle weave that you don't even know is there; the difference between 'random' and 'caused,' between illusion and truth, rhyming every reason.

Spiritual Rule 1: Be the river, not the dam. For the dam shall break, and the river shall run.

None of this writing or relative truth is 'mine.' This is but an excavation and curation of what always has been and always will be.

Hand-written letters are cool because they're clandestine; there's no digital trace. Plus they say: I took the time to physically write and print and mail this to you, because you mean something to me. As part of our re-humanization, I'd encourage a mass resurgence of penmanship and letter writing and a whole legion of Pen Pals passing the written evidence of love around the planet.

My job is to help direct the incoming tide.

The ego trip is fun, but full of hazards. After a while the urge is to let go and drift to the bank, else risk the cascade of self-realization.

It's not my reputation that matters. That's ego. Cancel away. It's the DIALOGUE that matters. It's the following of the signs and signals that the guide interprets, not the guide his/her self, for we're ever reborn.

The part of everyone that's most worth listening to is their philosopher. And everyone has one, whether known or not.

'Spiritual but not religious' means that you're sufficiently educated, intelligent and discerning to identify the spiritual truth in religious texts and discard the mind-controlling propaganda. All religious texts contain both, because they've all been corrupted by the egotism, greed and power of imperial history. SBNR means, in other words, that you realize that no one religion possesses an exclusive monopoly on spiritual truth or those whom speak it, thus enabling you to make good use of all texts. It means you can pass between the bars and in and out of the cages confining the religious, your heart and mind freed of artificial fetters.

The truth of Spirit is a strange thing. Like all truth, it's paradoxical in nature. It's simultaneously the most humbling and the most empowering of all truths. It's the knowledge of the everything leaning against nothing, the ego dissolving into egolessness.

Focus on WHAT you're eating, not how much. Get your quality right, then focus on quantity.

The most interesting people are never certain what they 'want to do with their life.' Everyone else suffers from a relative lack of imagination, thereby settling upon one self.

The ego is self-conceptualization and self-identification. It grows in inverse proportion to the spiritual truth of non-ego. And when you study ego, you find that everything that you append to your sense of self becomes its girth. Your profession, your religion, your politics, your nationality, your ethnicity, your possessions, your social media accounts, your relationships and on and on… they grow your sense of yourself until the shadow they cast overlords the truth of your spiritual nature: to be the One thing composing everything. This is why Fight Club states: "What you own ends up owning you," and why I and others consider the ego to be the shadow self that's cast when you place an illusively objective, separate self between you and the light of source Self. You're not the shadow, you're a condensation of the light. Slim yourself down to your most essential Self, jettisoning the inessential, and thereby approach God.

"May God be with you," the Christians say. But God is always with you, even if you deny it. "May you know your nearness to God," I say. May you understand Rumi's non-dualist refrain: "God is nearer to you than yourself."

Mortality is the form of formless immortality; the impermanent, forever adapting nature of God making matter for the infinitude of self.

People who live their entire lives in the safe comfort of boxes think of those living outside of them as somewhere between failures, insane asylum residents or reckless rebels. But to those living outside it, it's the BOX that's insane; it's a fabrication made to contain a sense of self that is never the truth of self, those believing it becoming insane. For how can one be sane when they believe in a reality made to contain them as if it's the one natural reality? Sanity is knowing your true nature, whilst insanity is believing that your nature is the unnatural containment.

'Being realistic' stands near to 'being dead.' Similarly, most of those fixated on 'being adults' or 'growing up' or 'being mature' are more like 'being servants' or 'staying small' or 'being brainwashed.' Break out of the boxes! You'll never know yourself whilst so artificially confined; you'll never live as your heart years for you to live. For I'd far rather die poor beside Walden Pond than live 'successfully' as a Trump in my tower.

If people work 'for you,' you're a exploitative, parasitic asshole. If people work 'with you,' you're an empowering, symbiotic humanitarian. If everyone that works together meritocratically shares in the bottom line, you're a progressive, and far greater than any of the 'for you' parasites feeding off of others. Because 'success' is actually adding value to life, in being the connecting, fertilizing river in facilitation of creating the greatest total quality of life. Failure is the dam that corrals wherewithal for the few, in desertification of total life.

If you think of people, planet and life as having value, and you understand capitalism and the stock market morally and relative to its effect upon the aforementioned, then capitalism (the taking of the value of the many and the planet to give to the few) and the stock market are simply the legalized theft of a corrupt legality that voids justice.

Thoughts don't come from you. You receive them relative to the focus of your mind.

Life sprouts from the ever bountiful middle, where the endless everything peels off of the never nothingness; where the eternal forever wars with the zero for the right to exist.

In the centermost passes One into the infinite, on the paradoxical plane of perfect possibility. The All Seeing Eye of One envisions all to come emanating from pitch black pupil through the iris of all potential to the all things sclera, the blackness of total condensation through every color of being to the infinite white and back.

All these irritants of mind coming from my ego and its self-inventions and self-defenses, from my body and its impulses and dependencies, its running away from pains and towards pleasures, from my environment and its incessant unnatural noises and heats and freezes and the endless throng of others vying for attention. Wash away all that I think I am, and the constant inundation in artifice and otherness, leaving but the truth of me.

Atop the forever flowing current of spacetime we careen into and collide with an endlessly shifting array of obstacles, bound in course by seemingly set shorelines, rapids perpetually rocking our conveyed sense of ourselves and our relationship to the turbulently overturning reality ever reflecting its transient truth off the surface of the water. Only in the quiet, shiftless undercurrent is there peace of permanence.

If 'normality' and 'sanity' are being well-adjusted to a capitalist society that wallows in greed, that forever suckles at the teet of instant gratification, that adulterates the planet and chronically consumes poisons and 'gets ahead' by exploiting his/her fellow human beings, then 'normality' is sickness, and 'sanity' is insanity. Moral human beings are necessarily maladjusted to the mental sickening of society. 'Fitting in' and 'being successful' can only define common failure.

One who lives in lies abhors the truth, and shall do everything in their power to make the truth-teller seem a liar, turn the spiritual into the heathen, and soil the immaculate.

Most of the undue suffering of humanity, that which revolves in the mind without progress, can be eliminated with mind control practices. Learn to identify where the thought is coming from, the source of anything and everything that enters your mind, and to encourage the sources that empower you whilst discouraging the sources that disempower you, while also spending time meditatively leaving the mind open to what wants to enter it naturally (the meditative state of the open vessel). When, for example, the impulse of the thought is coming from a physical addiction or dependency, or from an unhealthy, unnatural sense of need, or from the traumatized psyche or from the self-defending ego (the part of the mind that attacks others to feel better about itself), those things which weaken the self and cause one to worry and otherwise suffer, simply cut it off, refusing to feed it (refuse to deepen that channel), and then 'hold space;' hold your mind open, void and welcoming of something else to enter it, from progressive parts of the mind, such as from observation (presence/mindfulness) or the rational, spiritual and/or creative instruments of the mind. Learn to wipe the mind of the self-defeating thoughts by cutting them off at their source, through recognition and restriction of that source when such thoughts arise, through awareness of the source of the impulse of the thought, and to hold an opening, or 'negative space,' to be better filled. 'Mind control' thus best means controlling your *own* mind.

Compared to idealism, all else is cowardice and a combination of moral and imaginative failure.

Ask no questions, receive no answers, be led by the blind and greedy towards assumption and exploitation, conditioned to serve your inherited economic, moral and ideological masters. Yet, even following the ignorant, blind and greedy we may instinctively move towards the truth by pure faith and work, especially when done in the spirit of *service*.

Never forget that love and truth and their infinite manifestations and expressions are sanctioned by heart, for only there, at the gateway of Source to substance, may a divine sanctioning be announced; earthly powers may recognize and partner with it, but never may any of them be the sanctioning Source.

Don't get caught in the cages of convention and specificity, those are the traps laid by the conquerors. It's not about the specific words, the books, the symbols, the rituals, the categories, the classifications... but what they lead you to and make you feel and sense as inseparable from yourself. There are infinite pathways into the One. There are as many paths to the pinnacle as there are potential zigzags to be drawn from the broadest of all bases up to that transcendent peak, even as One guide leads you up all of them, and takes endless form of action, thought, embodiment and feeling through infinite heart. Release the false need of any specific pathway or guide, and fall upwards towards your peak.

Life is its own purpose. To experience it IS 'the point.' God is endless mortal experiences of immortal being, thus spacetime, energy and matter, the canvas created for the metaphysical rendering of endless existence.

Life is love is God. Spacetime, mind, matter, energy wrap around this core in Self-service. All are as finite forms set in service of the eternal Self; conveyances to and from One.

There's great irony in the fact that so many of us run, run, run from ourselves, seeking sanctuary from selfhood in the outer world. Yet we run from that which we carry with us, the restless, unsatisfied sense of self, while the only lasting sanctuary is in the innermost Self. Your outer environment affects your inner environment, but with faith and the meditative mindset it's the *inner* environment that determines peace. Even moving through tumultuous change and stress, the innermost is the only sanctum.

I'm a priest because I know I'm one with the One. I wish to provide a place of worship where every idea from every book, and every experience from every person, may elevate us; where controlling, disempowering specificity cannot overpower the inclusive empowerment of perfect generality.

Of the heart, believe into being.

Every prophet has a different message
revealed to them, as all light is affected
according to the lens through which it passes.

Only the
Silent
Stillness
Possesses
Perfect
Potentiality

Just say no, over and over again, to every presumption, every trained need, every element of your capitalist conditioning, continually denying the deniable, dropping the dependencies, wiping away the illusions of fixed reality until only the essential and necessary remains, to which we must say yes.

To the truly moral and spiritually awakened, God is the thread in the universal fabric wrapped around everyone and everything. To those pretending to be moral and leaning on one excluding religion, God is for tearing the fabric into as large a swatch of fabric as possible to be possessed and wrapped only around oneself and only those in one's tribe.

Don't believe western tradition. You weren't made to consume, to be comfortable, to work hard to enrich yourself and the tiny minority that owns most of the work at the cost of people and planet all so that you can possess a false sense of completion through your possession and position. You were made to know the One in the Infinite, to serve and enrich life, and therefore to full-heartedly serve God in all of Its manifestations.

On the other side of nothing is everything. I've been the everything from the nothing. I shall pass through the nothing to return to the everything, resettling into the illusion of a thing.

Food makes you weak unless it makes you strong. And it only makes you strong when it's called for; when it's strengthening and sustaining. Feeding the unnecessary is how unnaturality and weakness are made.

There's something so inescapably tragic about the life of the common-most contemporary, bourgeoisie existence: these embodiments of pure holy light caught in the semblance of existence, egoistically enslaved to the accrual of matter and the illusory class superiority imparted by its accrual as compared to every other tragically lost life. Wake up, else perish as an illusion of self.

Those who don't know and lack discipline tend to feed the evil simply because it's easier. More people do the wrong thing than do the right thing because it's easier to do so.

Strong sensations of heart are like creases in the metafabric.

I recommend that you masturbate as infrequently as possible. It's about the transfer and utilization of energy; about the retention and accrual of vital force. For there can be no denying the fact that, when borne by heart, the procreative act is at or near the height of the expression of life and love, and requires the release of a great deal of energy. This is the source of the expression 'petite mort.' Surely, then, gratuitously abusing the act without love in one's heart represents a great debasement, the cost of which is the corruption of body and mind commensurate with the dependency. For nothing is free; there's no action without equal and opposite reaction. All is either earned, paid for or stolen from the rightful possessors. You cannot consume the energy required of the peak physical act without consuming the vital force that compels the body, weakening you.

When you pray to God as though It's a 'he' that's 'above' and 'outside' and 'separate' from you, you know God not, and have yet to know in mind what God tells you in your heart. 'He:' God needs not the gender that is material only to material, physiological existence and reproduction. 'Above:' There's no above or below relative to the totality of spacetime existence. 'Outside:' There's no internal or external relative to the same totality of existence. 'Separate:' God is the most immanent of all immanence, as Rumi says: "nearer to you than yourself." The One in All cannot be separate from you, for it's the metaphysical constituent of physicality. Thus may you know the difference between the false, excluding, divisive, disempowering gods of religion made to control you and the true, perfectly inclusive, universally-uniting and empowering God that may set us free.

Meditating IS praying, because the innermost self IS Self, or God, and that's what meditation is about: dwelling in the quiet Self of non-mind. The masters may sit in Self even with mind, for those long-dwelling in Self may reduce their individualized sense of self to its slimmest, and so access mind with minimal psyche and ego, receiving pure, equanimous thoughts. A distinction between meditation and prayer only comes when prayer is corrupted by transaction, in paraphrasing Osho. If you're asking for something, if you're bartering with God as though you know better as to what is needed and why, and as though you understand better, *then* the schism is made between prayer and meditation. But this is not the true prayer.

Breathe through it, no matter what it is.

The Self sits in the perfectly equanimous, selfless center, the canvas of every painting.

Think only of servicing yourself, and all the trappings of false wealth shall come to you, and shall consume you with the same relish that you consume them. Think of servicing others, as brining greater life to life as a whole, and true, inconsumable wealth shall come to you, that which increases without bound, and expands the sense of self towards the terminus where self merges with the Self.

Practice listening, and observing in general. Nothing will increase your capacity to serve yourself and life in general more than your ability to and predilection for paying attention. Concurrently, nothing will free you from worry, greed and the ideas and defense of the small shadow self, or ego, like denying it through listening, observation, presence, service. Everything grows relative to consumption. Girth grows by the feeding.

Where lies produce profit and power, deception is popularity, truth is insurrection.

Look to the innumerable near death testaments for a clue as to what happens when the body perishes: you move towards the pure white holy light. What is such light? What is the perfect white? *Every color at once*. We come from the Everything, and we return to the Everything. From One into Infinite and back. As Huxley says in *Island*: "We've all come out of the same light, and we're all going back into the same light."

Mushrooms give me the Messiah Complex. Bring out your own inner messiah, I say.

The cost of the artificial online 'friendships' is the inhibition of offline real friendships, don't you see? The more energy and mental concentration given over to contrived connection the less there is for the true, spiritual thing. The natural, communitarian, spiritual human is being consumed by its avatars. In the vein of capitalistic divide and conquer Meta Monster murders mankind. May I post this to my Instagram account?

All-inclusive. Immanent-most, most eminent. That's what you're from, and shall return.

Finding God is like turning yourself inside out.

On mushrooms you sense the fallacy of words like 'accident' and 'random.' All is interlaced with absolute necessity, intertwined as free will and fate, all inseparable links in the causal chain, every moment a single domino in a cosmic game that's been played since before time first ticked, everything an essential player without which there would be no great game. Remove any domino, dominoes don't exist.

Is there anything more screwed up, more artificial, more against the natural social order and the universally-shared essential Self than proclaiming monogamous love to be superior? Evil incarnate are the ways of the conquerors, for the efficacy of conquering is always relative to its ability to divide and control. All may love all else, and yet the divide and conquer by which the capitalists control and oppress the human race is division in work, in possession, in socialization, even in love. It's all so clear. We've been indoctrinated in unnatural division, theologically, economically, politically, financially, socially, even in the spiritual interchange of love, where division is at its most unnatural. It's inescapable that salvation is relative to unification and the rule of love; the coming together to reclaim our humanity and spiritual nature, casting off oppression. We may remain our own person and have our own pursuits and pleasures and pains, but we may not remain divided without remaining sick, divided from our indivisible spiritual natures, and under the invisible yoke fools call freedom. This is why I make the distinction between relative individualism, which I call 'individualization' of the essential Self as a self, and the erroneous idea of absolute individualism. The former is freedom, the latter is enslavement.

I come into civilization and sicken. I accumulate what I require to run away. I flee into the forest to become well. I return for the means to retreat once more, sickening until the subsequent salvation. So goes the ceaseless cycle from sickening civilization to freeing forest. I must find a way to be self-sufficient in the forest, and forever be free.

The Devil is always chasing you. That's the purpose of the Devil: to compel you to run in the right direction, else lose the wars and be corrupted by the demons of every addiction.

Enlightenment is being exactly where you are in mind in body, without the least shred of the self-awareness of a Self-obscuring mind.

Those who don't understand the substance fall for the show, which, tragically, combined with the efficacy of propaganda and the prevalence of the egotistic illusion that more is more (as opposed to the truth that less of the invented you is more of the true you), explains the majority of human behavior.

Money is only meaningful within the manmade artificial constructs crafted for control. It has nothing to do with truth, meaning or purpose, or with the reason that you're alive. When money becomes your wealth, your life can only be impoverished.

Until 'working for' becomes 'working with,' until 'employee' becomes 'fellow owner-operator,' there can only be exploitation, injustice and the continued growth in every form of disparity, the makings of evil. We must systematically remake the economic system as a meritocratic cooperative constituted by what I call 'business collectives,' without which economics and finance can only serve the makings of evil.

The foundation remains regardless of the ruin precipitated by the godless greed of the egomaniacal monsters delivered upon people and planet. The freeing truth shall grow up from that foundation forever, regardless of the egos that believe they can conquer God.

The purpose of reading the right books is to mold consciousness; to hue, polish and dial-in the lens through which the pure holy light of Spirit passes into the individualization of the One Consciousness. 'Read the right books' is for the mind what 'administer the right medicine' is for the body. The brain is both.

Conquering is division is the killing of nature and the imposition of artifice. Divide humankind from our perfectly unitive, spiritual nature, and thus from God. Divide humankind from Mother Nature, and thus from our most natural foundation and inborn sense of symbiotic partnership. Divide humankind from itself and its fellow humanity by conditioning us to emphasize class and covetousness through our own misleading ego. Deepen these divides with perfectly dichotomous political parties and built-to-be-at-war ideologies. Now humankind isn't humanity, but is comprised of a perfectly mutually alienated collection of individuals, alone, afraid and confused, divided from itself, from one another, and from God. Individuals are weak and isolated and easy to dominate, subjugate, subdue, exploit and control. The innate, honor-bound duty of every moral philosopher, of every purified, spiritual theologian, and every truly progressive ideologue is to reverse the eons-old process of division and unify through perfectly universal, inclusive truths so as to free humankind from the conquerors.

When you accurately translate the Light of the Spirit as it passes through your conscious lens, you merge with every great thinker and writer ever extant; you become the sage in mind that everyone carries in heart. It's all about the merging; the point where all things become One; where infinite plurality punctuates your sense of your singularity.

Of all the insights offered by the double slit experiment, whereby the properties of light are altered by their perception, by how the light is experienced and measured, another is this: the Self is as the particle, the constancy of being, the self is as the wave, the changeability of being. By the properties of mind and body, by our state of mental and physical being, by our health, energy, mood and our relative state of stress or relaxation, and by the focus of our bodies and minds, we enact the wave. We vacillate up and down, amplifying or diminishing our separation from the Self (amplitude), being present as the Self or being elsewhere in our minds, concerned with our egos, seldom or often returning to our Self (wavelength), relatively heightened or oblivious in our awareness (frequency). When we don't perceive ourselves as a separate self we're closer to the particle, the ceaseless Self, and the extent to which we're aware of and concerned with ourselves as an individualization, as an egotistic entity, the more of the properties of the wave we enact. The goal of the consciousness may well be to be aware of and gain control of its waveform.

Walkabout means finding yourself by getting lost. Instead of being guided by the lies and controls of the conquerors conditioning conformity, throw away their corroding compass and wander by the inner compass leading to your Self; the Self cleaned of all of the artificial indoctrination and conditioning. It's the freedom of living without clock or calendar, aboriginally wise like *Crocodile Dundee*. You can't own what you come from.

The agony of passing through the Eye is the price of admission into the ecstasy; it's the painful process of rebirth bringing becoming.

The 'realist' lives in the illusion of a fixed and finite reality belying the truth of total fluidity. He's set himself in a cage he calls the truth, and sees the world through invisible bars invented by the warden to keep him under control. His reality consists only of forms and mechanisms, the how's divided from the why's, the reason separated from the mechanism, buying the illusion of random.

'Just say no' means far more than the Reagans could ever conceive of. In fact, it means the opposite of the particular fires that they stoked. They wanted you to say no to the drugs that free the mind, that support the counterculture that bids you drop out of joining the corporations and the military through which Raegan's puppeteers puppet and exploit people. In its far greater, freeing form, 'just say no' is the same as 'less is more.' It means denying everything false, misleading, oppressive and enslaving, leaving only the slimmest of customers empowered by the indispensable, universal and essential. There's no such thing as one way use. Everything is a double-edged sword. Everything that you use uses you in turn. Even those things that we think of as simply 'good' have a cost to their utility. Denying your use of them denies their use of you. The secret is to be as useful to as many people as possible without people using you in degrading ways; in ways that cost more to you than they're worth. To 'use someone' has negative connotations in the common lexicon, but the truth is that *utility* is a core concept that goes both ways, spanning the spectrum from parasitism to symbiosis, from using a slave to using one another for love.

Entitlement breeds supercilious monstrosity. When you're entitled to something that you didn't earn based entirely upon your means, your looks, being in demand by others etc., you have no appreciation for what you believe is yours by right, and you're ready and willing to destroy anything and anyone that impedes upon that right. Thus are the most monstrous people those whom feel the most entitled to that which others know must be earned, for only through the earning is there appreciation and value. Thus do the best people know that they're entitled to nothing, and are grateful for everything.

Everything exists for the sake of itself, as a causal necessity causing everything else.

The prevailing modern paradigm of realism-materialism-science pretends to circumscribe the entire sea of reality, when in fact it's but the surface-level view from above the sea, and hubristically dismisses the depths below, which constitute the majority of the sea. The modern cosmological paradigm is thus akin to the Titanic plunging towards the tip of the iceberg, imperiled by its surfacing of sight.

I retreat from society into nature for the same reason that I retreat from my egotistic mind during meditation: because God is easier to hear without added obscuring input.

'I don't get it' is the greatest of gifts,
forecasting the perfect joy of revelation.

Rivers distribute and redistribute the ocean.
That's the natural form. *Make me the river*.

The impulse to feed is arterial occlusion. It
impedes full, open flow and ushers in demise.

***

The 'male' is the progenitor, the procreator,
the disseminator, the innate desire to
reproduce. The female is the receptacle, the

matter-maker, the embodiment, the innate desire to cultivate. There's no point to one without the other. Deprived of Yin, Yang need not be. By the worship of the one to the other is the whole kept whole and holy.

The Gamemaster turns the game into that which seems of the gravest possible significance, then recycles it into new form.

Open the aperture by closing off the self.

Money is imprisonment pretending freedom.

Writing isn't what it seems. What the writer is ACTUALLY doing is hewing the relative consciousness of the reader; assisting them in crafting the lens through which they conduct their inner spiritual light through their minds.

Mushrooms are akin to Windows updating its software, except Microsoft is God, you're the software and nature's the hardware.

The brain receives and conducts
Consciousness as it passes through the body.

✱✱✱

The messenger is only as full as the vessel.

✱✱✱

Consciousness is like *Chutes and Ladders*.

✱✱✱

The first requisite of revitalization is the cessation of dissipation. This is why all modern, revitalizing diets are based upon excluding that which degrades the body. Everyone is clutching and cloying over illusions and shadows whilst the substance goes unnoticed. It's like the egotistic edifices that people build are forever set upon an fault line that must eventually topple them to the ground of being, forcing self-rediscovery.

You can't make a mark without putting yourself out there. Without risking what you believe that you are, you can never become.

Fiction is what you see. Truth produces what passes through perception to become fiction.

Let me explain a general moral military truth that seems to elude most Americans: generally speaking, the force that multiplies itself across the Earth so as to intimidate and leverage force, even before their invasions and occupations, is morally in the wrong.

Everyone prostitutes themselves one way or another in order to survive in modernity. The dictionary hides the commonality of contemporary prostitution as "capitalism."

Slavery didn't die. When you look at human history from the right angle it's clear that capitalism is simply the result of an evolving

concealment of slavery behind different
words and methods in resistance to progress.

If 'Israelite' truly means 'he who wrestles
with God' then I've always been an Israelite
without knowing it. We all are.

It's all about the internal environment:
cultivating your connection with your heart,
vitalizing and fortify the body and edifying
and controlling the mind. If you get your own
house in order, putting those three pillars in
place, you'll naturally remake your external
environment to reflect your internal
environment in your inestimable favor.

The longer that you hold the open vessel, and the more expensive that vessel, the more of the essential that may rush in to fill the void. And if you fill, you'll overflow to the benefit of everyone. This is called 'holding your cup up to the forever flowing fountain.'

Capitalism pays you when you only think about yourself and your tribe. God pays you when you serve everyone as if there is no self and no tribe. *Decide on your dividends*.

The originality of your ideas isn't what's important. That's all about your ego; the 'credit' that you desire for them. There's only so much truth, even as any truth can be expressed in an infinite number of ways. So it's no shock that thinkers of a similar mindset will come to the same conclusions across the history of spacetime. I once named non-duality 'monoexistentialism,' before I'd even heard of non-duality. The important thing is the value of the ideas in application to your life and the life of others; how life is served by those ideas. Very little, if anything, is perfectly novel. Everything is a re-creation, a re-composition, of what's always been and always will be, after all. What's novel is the unique way in which you look upon the idea, and the way in which you choose to apply it.

The synergy of knowledge and discipline is absolutely indispensable. Regardless of who you are and what you're capable of, without knowing what to do, and without knowing why, and without the will to actually do it, you can't be healthy and anywhere near to your full capacity, much less be best set to serve others. Any meaningful form of success requires the synergy of these two vital traits.

Nutrition is literal constitution of self. 'You are what you eat' isn't metaphorical, or some silly, meaningless remark. Without guarding against the consumption that reduces you and eating that which strengthens and protects you, especially in relation to the neuro-generative gut, you'll never know the complete you that you're meant to be.

There are three sources of evil. The first is caused through the temptations of the body; through pleasures which unnaturally reduce the self and create degrading dependencies and the false sense of need; i.e. physical and psychological addiction and enslavement. The second is caused through the temptations of the ego; through the illusion of a self and a group, or tribe, or family, as separate from and more important than any and all other selves, causing you to treat all 'others' as less deserving, thereby creating cutthroat conflict. The third grows from the second, and is caused through the temptations of possession and the illusion of ownership; through the greed that gathers more unto oneself and one's group, tribe or family than is necessary for the creation of their highest quality of life, especially when this greed deprives others of such. These three forms are always interconnected, and tend to gather force by the Snowball Effect.

'Good' is caused first and foremost by preventing evil. Thus, without knowing the forms of evil, how they tempt and how to prevent them, how can one be good? Becoming one's truest self, one's greatest good for oneself and others, requires building from the ground up, waging war against evil from body, to ego, to excluding ownership.

Love means connecting to what's truest; it's the essential-most in oneself connecting to the essential-most in someone or something, including oneself. In fact, it's been noted that connecting to the truest part of oneself is the very bridge by which we connect to the truest part of other people and things. Bridge-builders must love themselves to love others, else there's too great a gap to bridge.

Evil exists because it's harder to create and earn than to destroy and steal, and because ego and possession corrupt, and are easier to follow than heart and honor. Good exists because some are strong enough to do the harder thing. No good person needs the law.

Enhancing the experience of existence is innately purposeful, in parallel with both the practice of 'mindfulness,' of being as fully in the moment as possible, and with the misunderstood philosophy of hedonism, which actually runs parallel to mindfulness, and means: taking as much pleasure in things as possible, entailing the practice of fully presently absorbing them, not taking them for granted, noticing every subtle nuance. The greatest artists, cooks, lovers, and creators in general are thereby hedonists, with hedonism becoming a type of awareness, like meditation applied outward. Zen on the way in, hedonism on the way out.

Withholding from yourself makes you stronger, more resilient, less needy and dependent. Withholding from others makes you more desirable, because it seems as though you have something that they're unworthy of. So it is that great power comes from forbearance, and that every form of gratification is inversely proportionate to the indulgence of its feeding. You can use this knowledge to manipulate others as readily as you can use it to strengthen yourself.

The trick to being your most complete, healthiest self isn't to deprive yourself of the pleasure of eating. Such prohibition simply isn't sustainable for the vast majority, not to mention that it's unnecessary. The trick isn't to run away from food, but the opposite: to delve deeper into it. The trick is to learn the natural ways to increase food enjoyment, such as by your exploration of the vast realm of produce, spices and vinegars that most know very little of; to not need the unnatural forms of food in order for eating to be incredibly satisfying; to not be reliant upon just throwing sugar and salt and fat at food to be satisfied by it, but to be satisfied by natural flavors. By increasing variance and exposure to and practice in utilizing the near limitless cornucopia of natural foods and techniques, you can follow something like Paleo, Wahls or Whole 30 and lean yourself and heal your gut and become incredibly healthy without a hint of deprivation. It's a matter of knowledge, discipline and practice.

* * *

It's fascinating how things suddenly sound strange and purified on mushrooms. Like I hear someone accusatorially shout on TV "you need help!," like it's a severe rebuke of the subject, and I immediately think: Don't we all need help? Isn't that kind of the point of all legitimate spirituality and morality, solidarity, synergy and mutual reliance leading to understanding and love? A minute later I hear: "So you think they're on the honor system?," again as a type of condescension, like the subject is a fool for thinking that anyone would operate based upon 'honor,' and I immediately think: Exactly. The Honor System. What's been lost.

When the conquerors enslaved humanity, humanity rebelled against its enslavement. Gradually thus did the conquerors learn that they had to enslave without appearing to enslave, and so the dominant driving force of human history was triggered: building and leading humankind into mental, economic, political and religious cages that only a thin minority of the slaves have the discernment to clearly see; not nearly enough of them to convince the sightless slaves that they're real. THAT'S the heart of the human condition, always dressed up to look like something else: slavery slowly evolving in response to the pushback of progressives. Propaganda pretending to be truth. Enslavement feigning freedom. The 'free market' so called to conceal the fact that its entire purpose is to convince people to endeavor their entire lives to financially free themselves for the benefit of the conquerors. Plutocracy repurposing the republic because individual 'representatives of the people' are easy to target, corrupt and control in the cause of preventing popular progress for the sake of the same profiteering plutocrats pulling all the political strings, the result called 'democracy' so that the easy to train, gullible masses might more readily buy the show without the looking at the sordid substance.

The mind-controlling, narrow specificity of religiosity taking advantage of people's fear, doubt and dismay about divinity replaced the universally-empowering, freeing spiritual truth that we're all finite forms of the infinite One. How to set the people free? How to make them see? How to reveal the bars and walls of their traps to them? How to compel them to climb out of their cages? How to convince them to stop worshipping the false idols of ego, greed and the religious pretenses of God such that they might find their way out of divided and conquered modern parasitism and atavistically revert back to our interdependent, mutualistic, symbiotic spiritual nature, and be set free? It's my life-long response to this question that defines both my battle and my purpose.

The price of moral development is to be bothered by what others blithely skim over, unaware of the meaning and implications. Without outrage there can be no progress. Just don't let the outrage consume you. Be grateful for the holy *whilst* battling the evil manifestations of ego, tribalism and greed.

Don't try to impress anyone. They know when you're trying, and that trying isn't knowing or doing, but is found in the space between, in the liminal gap between desire and attainment, where doubt is keeping fiction from being fact. Impressing others will come naturally, as if by accident, when there's no trying, only enacting inspiration.

The more limited the mind the greater the need to classify in order to feign understanding; the more the need to categorize; to place in a box and say "see, I know what that is." Alas, the truth is that classifications are always relative, that almost no truth is absolute, and that our categorizations are therefore mirrors of our particular prejudices, and, thusly, very poor captures of but a fraction of the total truth.

For the enlightened, money is a river of love flowing without end, fertilizing the growth and potential of every form of life. For the conquered, money is but an emblem of ego, the dam that divides them from everything.

The reason for the gap reveals itself; the Spirit had to be impurified in order to know its purified form.

'Deeply' doesn't mean complexity, it means unobscured simplicity finally being revealed. The difficulty is in disentangling the countless overlapping threads, not making more knots.

It's my love for them that matters, not their self-mirroring assessment of me. If they fail to know and love me, it doesn't prohibit me from knowing and loving them. True love is unconditional, unless it's not, and not love.

The problem with Confucian philosophy is that everyone knows their place. Those that know it best are best fitted to, placed and stuck in their place. There's nothing given to the greater truth in between places and category; no room for the rebel that challenges proper placement for progress.

We so desperately need love that we'll create it as if from nothing, for from the nothing comes the most potent potential of everything. And when the mind opens itself to the full potential of the heart, we find that love can be found in everyone and everything, and we may gradually drop the clutching delusion of its limited association.

When I interact with a woman that impassions me, that demonstrates the perfectly balancing embodiment of my being, I sense an entire unlived love affair stretching out in front of us. And for that the modern mores and movements label me as 'creepy,' when in fact I'm the consummate romantic.

Falling in love is overlapping with the opposite; is Yin aligning with and balancing out its Yang; is purpose made personal.

***

In line with holism (the fact that everything is interconnected and that, therefore, separation is an illusion), herbalism always improves the whole body. Yes, specific herbs are best known for their effects upon specific systems of the human body, their 'affinity' for certain parts of the physiology, but most herbs not only impart a broad array of benefits across separately categorized physiological systems, but there's no way to improve any such system without simultaneously improving all the others, for they're interdependent. We may target certain systems and conditions, but the best herbal practice is to treat the whole, even before and in prevention of disease, for it's always the whole body involved. So it's about how herbs interact (their synergistic effect), their dosage, the variety of their use and how they're administered, not about whether or not any herbal medicine improves health.

The heart has no single home. No structure, no Church, no Synagogue or Temple can contain it, for it is of that which is contained within all. It's there that right and wrong and good and evil are distinguished, and where God grants sanctions, with no human authority required whatsoever.

I refuse to worship Mammon with my work, as most secretly do by nature of the system that they serve. He hides himself in the foundation of the capitalistic construct upon which they build, all built upon his patronage. At least the Devil worshippers are honest about the fact that they serve the same lord that most Christians bury in their basements, serving him with their actions whilst denouncing him with their words.

Write, whether right or wrong, whether read only by oneself, or by the masses whom we move. For we grow by the pen more than by any other implement, regardless of appraisal.

The forbidden flower always smells sweetest. What need have we for all the equally fragrant flowers we daily crush underfoot like daffodils? 'New' is relative to paying attention. Every daffodil is different. The fact that those on the other side of the fence appear more beautiful is your covetousness, reflecting your lack of appreciation, which, in turn, is a reflection of insufficient attention.

Don't wait until you're ready.
Let the doing of it ready you.

Every male ego, likely every ego, is led by one dominant drive: to prove to itself and others that it's the alpha male. The more insecure and closer to boyhood the male, the truer this is. How ironic is it that the very need to prove the potency of manhood is the same thing that demonstrates the lack thereof.

The term 'pedestrian' has drummed up some negative connotations, but really there's little better than exploring the world on foot, as we naturally evolved, vagabonds to the last of us. The fact that this connotation is steeped in the assumed supremacy of 'advancing' transport technologies is telling.

You can't truly hear until you quiet your mind. You can't truly see until you see without self.

When one's posts and project promotions are continuously censored ('cancelled' or 'rejected') by mega corporations like Meta and Amazon perpetually pandering to the profitability that perfectly piggybacks upon political correctness, the first reactions are anger and frustration. Then the revelatory second reaction dawns: it's a sign that I'm telling the truth, and must therefore be one of the few on the right track, pulling away from the masses mentally conditioned by corporate conquerors, offering them truths threatening the control of those conquerors.

It's a well-known fact that people live longer, experience a greater quantity of years, simply by consuming less; only according to need. It's a little known fact that people live better, experience a greater quality of years, knowing that 'consuming' means far more than food, and what they need most is thereby revealed. In a slight revision of a famous quote from the nineteenth century, to make it more universally considerate, inclusive and valuable: "Tell me what you consume and I'll tell you what you are."

This will sound counterintuitive, but whatever the problem, whatever the challenge, it's always best to face it head on. *Go right at it*. Take the most miserable, direct path. Trying to avoid it or to more comfortably circumnavigate it only sustains the problem, delaying a solution until you find the strength to turn around and face it. It's like being at sea and being beset by a potentially capsizing storm. You must pass *through* the storm. You must face it and fight your way up until you crest its mightiest waves. Trying to go around it will capsize you horizontally. Trying to run from it means that it'll eventually crash down on top of you. Only by staring it straight in the teeth and bearing what it forces you to bear may you know the blue sky on other side of the storm.

'Fasting' and 'cleansing,' like all practices in abstention, selectivity and self-control, possess five priceless benefits desperately needed by modern mankind: (1) *Mind Control*. Instead of being led by bodily impulses and all the connected weakening

corruptions and dependencies that may be incurred upon and spur the body, you're declaring that your mind shall instead control your body. This prevents your being enslaved to the body, and is an indispensable step in acquiring the rarity of positive freedom.
(2) *Revitalization*. Most of the unnatural stress that we self-destructively incur upon ourselves is based upon consuming too much, especially unnatural, unnecessary substances that beleaguer us. By taking the demand off of the body, you allow it to utilize its energy in cleaning, fortifying and healing its systems. (3) *Planetary Protection*. Everything destructive delivered upon Mother Earth is based upon humanity's unsustainable exploitation, consumption and pollutive discharge of its limited resources. By not contributing to the unsustainable evils of capitalistic consumerism, you protect Her.
(4) *Economic Impact*. By not contributing to the demand of unhealthy, corrupting,

dependency-inducing commodities (like processed food, pharmaceuticals, narcotics and pornography) that fuels their supply, you help reduce the power and profits of their suppliers and the impact that those suppliers have on everyone. (5) *Spiritual Enrichment*. By finding the strength to give your body the low demand time to rejuvenate itself, and by becoming a lean, mean 'slim customer,' you simultaneously learn what true need is, and thereby drawn nearer to the essential-most within you, that which has no need: God.

It's a little known but fundamental moral law that it doesn't matter if you're right or wrong. Those are the egotistic concerns of the shadow self. What matters is the effect you have upon people, the planet and life in general, including yourself. Those are the enlightened concerns of the essential Self. Right and wrong are relative to the best interests of the whole of life and the planet.

Indignation isn't healthy or productive in and of itself. Don't get stuck there. It has to be transmuted into the solutions to have value.

Negative freedom paves the path to enslavement to one's weakness, descending into Hell. Positive freedom reveals the path to freedom from one's weakness, ascending into Heaven.

Everyone is self-interested. That's simply the nature of being a self. The question is whether or not that self-interest is of the type that cooperates with or that conflicts with the self-interest of others; the extent to which it's exclusive or inclusive, symbiotic or parasitic. The answer to this question also answers the extent to which the self-interest is right or wrong, and conducive to love, solidarity and universal spiritual identity (the nature of God) or hate, conflict and individualist and tribalist egotistic identity (the nature of Satan). These are the battle lines in the ongoing war of good and evil.

What's in a name? More designation, classification and control than truth and justice. Everyone wants to know what to label the person or thing so that they can assuage their egos that they understand it and have put it in its proper place. Very few realize that this constant egotistic exercise of stuffing things into constricting boxes conflicts with the spiritual, moral and greater intellectual exercise paralleling Oscar Wilde's universal aphorism: *to define is to limit*.

In a land of overabundance in which the food supply is dominated by the unscrupulous daily selling the wellbeing of their patrons for profit, selectivity of intake is the only thing separating your diseased self from your truest, alive self.

Self-righteousness is confusing vanity for morality.

Spirituality is the instinct towards and practice of escaping one's self in the merging with the One Self, finalized in the death of the self. During the life of the self, this is achieved by sinking internally into and harmonizing with the deepest core of the self where the Self sits upon Its eternal throne. Sinking into the Self remains the spiritual quest regardless of the extent to which the self physically and mentally moves through a universe produced by the One Self expanding into infinite selves. So it is that while everything in existence is a version of the One Thing (non-dualism), the nearer we are to our essential Self within *while* we move without, the clearer our sight, and the purer the truth of our observations of the outer. For the outer is a projection of the inner, and nearness to our innermost Self allows us to be nearer to the truth of everything without.

Presidents, prime ministers and politicians in general would only be leaders if democracy were real; if the people gave them their power directly, and willingly, unfiltered by the parties and powers corrupting and dis-authenticating democracy. But the world is run by the wealthy and powerful puppeting the politicians from behind the scenes, hence the proper term for the majority of political systems: plutocratic republic. The puppets aren't the leaders, they're the front; the show to distract, mislead and conceal the real leaders: the puppeteers hiding their strings.

The less secure the inner self, the greater the need to appear secure outwardly. The more glittering and overblown the show the more insubstantial and impotent the substance. Substance makes no show of itself.

Truth is the enemy of those profiting from lies.

Your reaction to the less fortunate is a litmus test of your morality. If, for example, you encounter a homeless person and react with revulsion and condescension, keeping as far away from them as possible, you're likely relatively supercilious, classist, egotistical and morally undeveloped compared to someone whose reaction is one of compassion and the desire to empathize with what landed them there, and to help alleviate their misery.

The goal of social liberty is to have ongoing access to the best and most varied of human society whilst never being subject to any of it.

The greater one's moral development and authentic conviction the more that pleasing others represents compromising oneself. Thus it is that the popularity and 'success' that comes from people-pleasing necessitates the selling of oneself and the sacrifice of honor and morality for the true progressive champion. One cannot be a champion of the people truly serving the best interests of those people whilst compelled to popularly please them, for that which is in their best interests is seldom what they're comfortable with, and that which confirms their egos and worldview, but is usually that which uncomfortably challenges them to see the injustices that they're programmed to ignore, to expand their worldview, and to grow past the confines that society imposes upon them.

While seen as an absolute positive by most, what's considered 'knowledge' can often be restrictive, and, thus, an impediment. Any form of 'knowing' which mandates that there's but one way to think or do things thereby narrows the thought and activity of the learner that believes it. This is especially true when it comes to anything creative, or requiring of the uninhibited, open, seeking mind. This is why, as examples, we have Yoda's "you must unlearn what you've learned," why some companies disqualify those with too much or certain types of education or experience, why the 'spiritual but not religious' thinker is reduced by being exposed to too much dogma from any particular religion, why someone naturally inclined towards philosophical thought might choose to think and write without studying previous philosophers, and why some writers choose not to learn all the rules of the language(s) in which they write so that they write as naturally and creatively as possible, rather than worrying about keeping inside of proscribed lines. Not to mention the even more obvious example of modern western society being an ongoing act of conservative, consumerist, capitalist indoctrination which grossly inhibits its members from thinking in ways that progress beyond and free people from such paradigms. The goal of progressive education must therefore be to liberally exercise the mind and offer it endless perspectives and tools, rather than stifling it with mandated, inhibiting types of thought.

Enlightenment isn't something you *attain*, like climbing a spiritual ladder from some base animalistic being to becoming the Buddha, and thereby 'escaping the cycle of death and rebirth.' Ironically this not only underestimates the gift of life and the purpose of One into Infinite of One (represents an ignorance of the metaphysical construct), but is an egotistic interpretation of the antithesis of egotism: the practice of spirituality: the release of the egotistic small self in order to experience existence as the egoless Self. In truth the enlightened Self exists within the egoistic self at all times, with 'moments of clarity/enlightenment' experienced when the obscurity of the ego is pierced, or lifted, under certain conditions, such that only the essential Self remains. This is called "piercing the veil" or "lifting the veil," and is something everyone experiences. The goal of meditation, whether as an activity or, better, as a practiced state of mind applicable to every moment, a type of 'indwelling' as we move through existence, is to return and sit in this state as much as possible. Enlightenment, in other words, is our natural state, and is obscured by the ego;

the thoughts of the self as separate from the Self which act to cloud the clarity of our sight.

The key to success is seeing everything as an opportunity; seeing the potential for 'yes' whilst not focusing your mental energy on every 'no' that you hear. The 'yes' and the 'no' are always there; it's simply a matter of which of the two you focus on and follow.

Pain and suffering are nature's way of offering you lessons. Most people don't learn them, concealing the pain and suffering with fleeting pleasures and distractions, growing the false sense of self in service to Satan, the master of greed and ego. A select few prove themselves worthy by learning and applying the lessons, enduring the required pain and suffering and thereby slimming the false sense of self, the master of lies, thereby drawing nearer to Spirit, the master of truth.

Corporations are a legal means by which people can commit crimes. Their purpose is simply to create a legal entity that takes the fall for the wrongdoing of its shareholders, insulating those shareholders from legal responsibility for their trespasses upon people and planet. They allow for, as two examples, creating weapons and 'security forces' that kill with impunity overseas on behalf of the military industrial complex, or stealing from the people through abuses of the financial system and the immorally intertwined real estate market. You should refuse to patronize or work for them on this principle alone, that the purpose of their design is to prevent legal recourse for the crimes that their owners and operators commit, even before getting into their contribution to every unsustainable socioeconomic and environmental evil endured by the planet and the whole of life.

One of the keys to happiness is learning how to love not only unconditionally, but without needing to possess who and what we love. For as soon as there are conditions to our love, that love is adulterated, and loses its genuineness. And as soon as we're compelled to possess what we love we inflict the evil of trying to keep them/it from others, denying others their love for them/it, while also opening ourselves to the pain of losing the love we can never truly possess; for ownership of anything is an illusion, when everything we are and gather unto ourselves must inevitably perish, returning to the source from which all love springs. Thus, love unconditionally, without possession, being grateful simply for the time that you have to feel and express that love. It's a *very* difficult practice as, like all the most worthwhile practices, it requires not listening to your ego, which shall bid you to possess and control everything that may benefit you.

Any movement any one direction is a movement away from every other direction. Any thought about anything is a denial of any other thought about that thing. Any professing of knowledge about anyone or anything is a refuting of any contradictory knowledge. Any definition, categorization or classification is a box into which nothing can ever perfectly fit. Thus, only in the thoughtless center, without preconceived notion, without category or definition, without bias or objective, without judgment or qualification, is there the truth of the complete possibility of anyone or anything. Knowing this state of pure, unrestricted possibility out of which anything and everything can be created and will forever be re-created is the same as knowing the divine state. Sitting in this state is sitting in the heart of God, in which all may be known and loved.

People don't want the truth; it's too inconvenient and unpopular. People want to be able to say that they know the truth-teller.

✳✳✳

The soul is an invention of religion used to control the mind and actions of the believer. There's but one 'soul,' one immortal essence, what I call Spirit, and everyone and everything is an inseparable aspect of it. But if a religion can get you to believe that you possess an immortal essence separate from everyone and everything else's, then they can enslave your mind and take charge of your will by convincing you that they can, in the most common religious propaganda, 'save your soul' and permit its passage into Heaven, and prevent its passage into Hell, neither of which actually exist. For, again, there is no separation at the base of being, and you're not separate from Spirit or any of Its facets, so there is nowhere to 'go after you die,' because you're already forever there.

Scientists, realists, materialists and atheists are so fixated on the how and the what that they've neglected the all-important why. They're locked into the forms, entirely ignorant of the formless source of every form. The religious make a different critical mistake: believing the formless takes an exclusive form, when It's perfectly protean.

There's something inherently unnatural and unhealthy about monogamy, much less marriage; a desperate need for stability and control. Regardless of how much you love one another, that co-dependency breeds resentment; a need to be less confined, and truer to the innate endless possibilities of an existence which you cut yourself off from. There's no way to peer through a telescope, regardless of how splendid and pleasing the view, without needing to know what's outside it, and without having malice for the telescoping aspect of the telescope. This explains what's wrong with everything exclusive and confining, including not just marriage but all the masters of modernity: science, religion, realism and materialism.

All wisdom comes from 'what do you need?,' not from 'what do you want?' All strength comes from 'and if I refuse?,' not from 'what do you want from me?' Alas, all peace and cooperation come from: 'what can we do for one another?,' not 'why are you in my way?'

Need sickens. Gratitude is salvation.

You bequeathed me a self, so I try to preserve it, because it's all that I know. Desperately, I clutch it, as somewhere deep inside I wish it weren't so. And the tighter my grip upon it, the less that I can see your light, which is like the firefly in my clenched fist.

There's a momentary sense of panic when attempting to crest any wave. After the anguish, you simply turn around and ride it.

***

Less animal. More plant. Caveman good.

***

Modern medicine classifies some of the strongest medicines as 'poisons.' Ask yourself why that is so, then watch the rabbit run. Don't fall too deeply into the burrow Alice!

***

The less that you force your body and mind to process, the more you'll process yourself.

Confidence and charm aren't 'qualities,' they're powers.

I'm a disciple of the Golden Teacher. And I give thanks to Ra, our Father. He gave us not just light and the warmth that gave rise to all of life in all of its forms in holy communion with our eternal Mother Earth, but He daily shines with a life-giving, energy-offering force that guides in countless waveform languages. And we the wise few listen, and seek to plant His offerings into Mother Earth, and, with Her blessing, cultivate them until they overgrow the boundaries, the symbiotic supersession such that life once again grows into itself.

Taking mushrooms is Playing Emperor.

Who was it that said: "To find out who rules over you, find out who you're not allowed to criticize?" Voltaire, I believe. I might reword this as: "To find out who's of most value, find out who's being monitored and 'cancelled.'" I figure if you're not being actively monitored and censored you're not doing your job as a servant of the peoples' awakening.

Fasting is fun. It's a challenging exercise in self-control that strengthens body and mind.

There's only one true measure of courage and heroism: doing and saying what you think is right and in the best interests of the greatest number of your fellow lifeforms regardless of the ramifications for you.

I watched a lizard pursue and consume a grasshopper, and realized that, for Spirit, it's just a transfer of energy between Its forms, the transfer based upon environmental pressures eternally pursuing equilibrium.

Taking mushrooms is like receiving a conditioning and comb-through treatment for your consciousness. The cleansing and knot-tearing disentanglement are uncomfortable, even potentially painful and frightening, but the increase in the quality of consciousness is well worth it, and reinforces a fundamental lesson: Improvement is uncomfortable, because it's about leaving your stagnating comfort zone. If you spend your time making sure you're always comfortable and secure, you'll never grow. If you too long fixate upon and invest in a specific version of yourself, you'll never discover all the unrealized versions of yourself, for, in our hearts, in our essence, we're like Proteus: able to become anything.

Don't use credit cards. They use *you*. It's a scam to prey upon people's desperate desire to live beyond their means; a scam that's paid for by having parasites attached to your flesh for life, absorbing as much of your limited means as they can whilst preparing to reduce your self-esteem by belittling and relentlessly pressuring you into submission should you fall behind. The cost of credit is financial and psychological enslavement and reduction. The fact that it's the most common of scams doesn't change that. Pay them off then cut the leeches from your flesh! Then do the same with your work and your home, putting yourself in the position to own them! Own them, else leeches own *you*!

I'm against credit cards, leases, corporations, the stock market, the 'defense industry,' our sham 'democracy,' pharmaceuticals, fast and processed food, concentrated animal feeding operations (CAFOs), religion and marriage. Why? Because I'm one of the few that knows what they cost the vast majority of people. They're forms of parasitism and divide and conquer. They're tricks designed by the exclusively advantaged to take advantage of the disadvantaged lack of insight and inclusion. They're akin to bars in the entrapping cage and links in the chains shackling us to the servitude hiding behind the lie of freedom through which the profiteering propagandists leech off of us. Until the majority understands this as very few do, until the majority fully realizes the extent of the problem embedded in the foundation of unsustainable, inevitably crumbling western society, the people will continue to trudge through life as victims blind to the blood-sucking leeches plastered all over the skin of society. Until we band together and pool our collective buying power to buy our freedom, we're slaves!

Once you understand the full implications of the accounting equation, you understand everything that you need to know about 'business ethics.' There are three columns. To the corporation you're either an asset to be sucked off of as much and for as long as possible, or you're a liability to be minimized and discarded. You're never in the equity column, the only one sharing the bottom line.

How do you know when it's a lie? When it empowers the few at the expense of the many. How do you know when it's true? When it empowers absolutely everyone the same way. Such is the relativity of truth always measured by the relative universality of its application to the people and planet.

True spirituality is never 'other.' Rather, it's about the very illusion of otherness. It's never about 'another' time or place, or about 'another' realm of the afterlife for the ego-based 'soul,' or about including some and excluding 'others.' It's never about the tribe, it's always about the whole. It never, ever says 'these are the chosen people,' it says 'all of life is equally divinely-manifested, and all are your holy brothers and sisters.' When you come to truly sense the all-inclusive, all-encompassing interdependence of Spirit, you know that no one and nothing is excluded, and that spacetime and matter constitute the existential construct allowing Infinite of One. Religion and science fail their followers by failing to find this foundational truth, making divides and enforcing separations in the essentially indivisible and inseparable.

Religion was the first corporation. Why? What are corporations built on again..? That's right, taking advantage of disadvantage so that the privileged few can take advantage of you. D&C 101: Keep the people divided from one another, and from sharing in the sweetest, equity-based fruits of owning their work and being included within God. Only then shall they remain disempowered and weak enough to be parasitically sucked from.

Why is it that when I stir a soup in its pot it looks exactly like the universe? Does the alchemist enlist the same cosmic forces?

Reality is an interchange between self and Self. If you believe that you're an independent being you're still at the starting blocks, else running the race with a blindfold.

When you're playing with the whole deck, you don't need to 'make a play.'

The truth of it is in the feeling, not the thought. The thought comes after and piggybacks upon the feeling, like energy that must enter the wire before illuminating the bulb. That's what the scientists, atheists, realists and materialists will never understand: *Sense* is the unqualified quintessence of what the mind grasps at.

Order of operations: heart, spinal cord, brain.

The foremost sign of intelligence is the ability to turn off the mind; to realize that all of the paddling belies the purpose of the current.

Every ego recognizes every hollow victory of pride. Every heart recognizes every substantive victory of love.

You know you have someone beat logically when they start insulting you. No one that's confident in their reasoning has any need to distract and emotionally upend their opponent. You only attack the ego and emotions of your opponent when the mind has secretly lost the battle, as per the Ancient Greeks' three modes of persuasion, and the way in which demagogues rule: pathos and ethos are enlisted to conceal a loss of logos.

The less adulterated by man, the better. For man knows but the artificial fabrication of the forms and features of the divinity that nature knows and bestows innately, and the best of man is defined by his and her refusal to sell out his fellow man by doing any less than partnering with and evoking natural divinity.

The secret purpose of the two party system is for the two sides to cancel one another out so that no true progress can be made for the people, in order that the profiteering, plutocratic status quo be maintained whilst the façade of democracy conceals the fact that the actual governance continue in hushed, closed-door meetings amongst the monied whom continue to unsustainably carve up people and planet. It's all so that those at the table can continue carving up the people and the planet on the menu. That's what American 'democracy' *really* is.

True belief is inseparable from the product of reality. It's mind into matter. Which is why 'confidence is king:' it reigns over reality, imposing its will upon it, all its subject.

Masters are made not by infallibility, but by having made, and learned from, every lesson offered by every mistake there is to make.

The most common mental prison is the belief that you always have to be 'doing something.' Ironically, you only begin to explore consciousness and discover what you're capable of when you realize that there's no such thing as 'doing nothing,' and that physical and mental stillness allow for 'doing anything.' For the whole may only ever enter the most expansive of empty vessels.

I left myself behind so that I could walk ahead. The weight was too great.

The battle is over before it begins, fought between those whom have conquered themselves and that which they conquer.

Until you know yourself completely, in your deepest rooted essential Self indivisible from totality, you're vulnerable to what others say that you are, and to what your fear tells you that you are. The self is vulnerable relative to its awareness of itself. Where it's ignorant of itself, only there may fear and doubt assail it. Opinion sticks to the shadow, not the true self. The deepest, truest Self is certain of itself; of what it is and what it isn't. It can't be convinced that it's something that it isn't, for lies only stick to the self. Only the ego, the shadow of the true self, can hold limiting, negative and reductive ideas of itself, and suffer by it. Thus is peace a product of Self-knowledge, the ability of the self to see its shadow and know that it's a projection of the Self passing by one window of perception.

Peace is a product of Self-knowledge. Suffering is a product of Self-ignorance. All forms of Self-ignorance are thus as painful stones walked on the path to Self-knowledge.

Words are like signposts. They can guide you as to which way to go, but they can never constitute the path. The Tao is innate, the words pointing to inroads of Self-revelation.

***

Relative to the spiritual Self the self is like a skin cell, forever sloughed off and remade.

***

God is the reality of selflessness constituting the inseparability of existence. God's work is the unitive work of love stitching inseparability. Satan is the illusion of independent self constituting the perception of separable existence. Satan's work is the divisive work of ego evoking the unstitching of separation. They are the Yin and Yang of metaphysics, each fundamental to the metaphysical fabric. There can be no sense of the one without the other, for to be aware of the fabric is to be aware that the fabric may be torn to pieces. Yet, no matter how many and how small the pieces, it's the nature of the fabric to be whole and indestructible. Burn it to ashes, and the ashes reassemble.

You represent God relative to your ability and willingness to speak universally inclusivist truths; truths equally applicable to everyone and everything. You represent Satan relative to your illusory need to speak exclusivist lies; lies applicable to exacerbating the sense of separation and division that brings advantage to the excluding and disadvantage to the excluded, oppressing everyone by inhibiting the unitive truth that'll most empower them.

I offer you one of the most important, most difficult lessons that you could ever learn: Place no stock in people's judgment of you, only your own. Why? Not only can they only perceive what they see and can comprehend of you, and can they thus never known the whole you, but people's ability to judge is so poor that they elected president the most absurd clown to ever disgrace the stage.

Life is about being on the wave as it crests. The experience of cresting matters most.

Where a leader is needed, a leader steps forward. A leader needs no more cause.

No matter the perceived power of the person, they can only ever have as much power over you as you allow them to. Such is the nature of true power: *it's given willingly*, because those that give it know that it will empower them in turn. When power is made by force or deception it may only be detrimental, and may only last until the point of being met by a greater force, or by the revelation that wipes away the deception.

***

A man whom has yet to take control of the base drives of his sensual nature is no man at all. He is like a boy whom has yet to saddle or pen his horses, and is thus continually trampled underfoot whenever they run wild.

***

Masturbation enslaves you to the sexual impulse. It conditions the body and brain, the nervous system and psyche, to need sex regardless of the social and spiritual catalysts which serve to naturalize it, creating debilitating dependency, the weakened, needy body and brain enslaved to sexuality.

EVERYTHING matters. There's not a single thing that doesn't factor into play upon and within Consciousness, regardless of your awareness. That's the thing about the truth: it's careless of opinion. At the same time, the truth you hold within your portion of Consciousness, your opinion, determines you.

It's all just one big cross-species territorial display. Until… you take yourself outside that zone, and learn how controlled you've been.

If you've never experienced psychedelics, you exist within a cage you're unaware of, and that can never be precisely described to you.

Very few of us feel the shackles so acutely that it doesn't matter how much the world tries to convince us that they're not there, and when we point to them, that they're there for our own good, and for the good of everyone else. Our purpose is to expose and remove them, and not just from ourselves, but from the whole world of soft, softly suffering slaves who have yet to see them.

Big Self equals small self minus belief. That is, the ONLY thing preventing you from knowing and being your limitless, unrestricted self is the belief in your limitations and restrictions. Those limitations and restrictions are mostly a product of a society designed to profit off of you, and NOT by your nature, or for your benefit. Everyone feels and its aware of this to various degrees, defining the spectrum of potential rebel leaders to potential rebel soldiers. But make no mistake, the rebellion is real, and has existed for as long as one ape started imposing limits on another, tricking him into believing the limits were his nature.

Where society itself is in the wrong, civil disobedience is the same as honor.

Profit is successfully selling to unsustainable human weakness and dependency. The more profitable business is, the weaker and more dependent becomes the humanity set upon the more quickly destabilizing planet. Period.

Social acceptability is about fear, programming and control. Propriety is about sheep bred to be sheared for their wool, penned into artificial existences and slowly being slaughtered, never having lived.

Healing is about two things: (1) reducing towards elimination all unnecessary demand (2) increasing towards maximization all necessary supply.

Do you not see that money is simply slavery hiding as currency? Total independence via communalism is the only way to be free.

The challenge isn't to fill the empty space, but *not* to fill it; to not plaster something over the divine walls of the silent, eternal edifice.

The heart is the gateway; the entry point of the pure conscious energy of Spirit into matter. And the same cognitive neurons that are in the head are also in the heart. So when you follow your heart, what're you following?

Honor is heart bound to mind.

I want one thing above all else: to empower the people to know their true selves, and thereby summon the collective strength to overcome the oppressing exclusivist class that feeds off of their invisible enslavement.

Good and evil aren't separate things. They are two parts of the same whole. Every Yin has its Yang, because the One is made of the many. Stories are invented to justify the existence of something that was made as an equal and opposite reaction to the One, as if Evil exists in some ones and not in other ones. Yet everyone possesses the perpetual possibilities of both, as there can't be the limitless potential of the void without the possibility of it being filled, just as white is all the colors coming from black, the absence of color. You can't produce infinity except from nothing. In this existence, the Devil is the symbolic justification for the side of the coin that we don't want to belong to us; the patsy; the excuse that we substitute for a truth that we can't conceive of or accept. Evil doesn't exist by itself, for the sake of itself, exclusive of Good, but is a byproduct of the vulnerable nature of the body and the mind that evolved

from the immortal One expanding through
the Big Bang to become an infinity of ones.

There's this story that one of the head angels,
Lucifer, rebelled against God because he was
evil and was cast out of Heaven for his sin,
with a third of the angels following him,
thereby becoming demons. The truth: 'God'
was the oppressive emperor, and 'the Devil'
rebelled against him, with a third of the more
progressive aristocratic heads of state
following. They lost the rebellion and were
outcast. It's called 'propaganda,' people!

When the few possess something that the many don't and use it to control and profit off of them, whether it's force, religious authority, money or some other form of excluding empowerment, the people suffer from that particular mode of slavery. No people can truly thrive when their entire lives are subject to any type of excluding control.

Never forget that the ego of all but the most secure people drives them to attempt to reduce who you are and what you're capable of in order to feel better about themselves; to make you feel smaller so that they feel commensurately bigger. This is the primary motive of most forms of human interaction.

Every self perishes, even as the Self is eternal. Thus is all goodness glorification of the Self, even in sacrifice of self, and is all evil glorification of the self, in sacrifice of Self.

Ego and greed come from caring less.
Holiness and truth come from caring more.

The most effective form of activism is the disciplined refusal to purchase products and services that profit from evil and suffering. If you refuse to demand, the supply must die.

Profit, like evil, is based upon exploiting and encouraging human weakness and planetary unsustainability. Good is based upon reinforcing and encouraging human strength and planetary sustainability. Man vs. Nature. Only when man returns to nature shall the prevalence of insane unsustainability end.

The failings of modern mental health treatment are the same as all modern health treatment failures: isolated symptom over systemic cause. The patient is isolated as the 'sick individual' and the 'sickness' is blunted with chemicals that don't fix but only conceal and exacerbate the root systemic causes. So the sick just become sicker and dependent upon concealing chemicals that heal nothing. In fact, all modern issues can be seen through the treatment lens of narrowly symptomatic inefficacy vs. broadly systemic efficacy. The treatment of the whole human race and the ailing planet is sitting on this fulcrum of systemic success vs. symptomatic failure.

The most mature people always have fun.

Pride is compensation for insecurity. Self-knowledge is the path to confidence. Self-love is the path to salvation.

***

The more insecure the person, the more that their ego is invested in their reality.

The path to self-security goes through the land of insecurity. You have to pass through the fear evoked by the insecure, smaller self in order to draw nearer to the bigger Self.

Christ is the open channel of the heart; the conduction of the pure white light through the perfectly polished lens. No embodiment of Spirt needs religion. Religion is but the curation and confinement of the eternally conducted light. All who know Spirit know that they may sample from any conduction, regardless of source. For all is sourced from the One Source, and Christ never intended that Empire should make him into a religion.

No society that fails to serve its most needy and disadvantaged members, that does not actively approach and attempt to render compassionate service to the suffering, may look into its mirror and call itself 'advanced.'

Every uncommonly realized truth that flies in the face of one or more common lies is 'politically incorrect.' Therefore, the cost of absolute fealty to political correctness is to betray the truth and support lies and injustice relative to the rational incorrectness of the political correctness in question.

Those that don't understand the argument are taken in by those putting on the greatest show of understanding the argument. That is, those that don't know the substance are consumed by the show, such that a majority thereby consumed is inevitably ruled by the circus, clowns concealed by presidencies.

When time flows over you, unfelt, you're of the One. For time is measured only by the forever changing self belying the changeless.

The whole sits in the center, and is always satisfied by its nature. The fraction orbits around the whole, and is unsatisfied by the nature of being incomplete, uncentered and forever unsettled in its ceaseless motion.

What always matters most is your internal environment. Until you're intrinsically aligned, the extrinsic is mostly irrelevant.

Only one who knows evil intimately is well equipped to fight it; not the pretense of evil, read of in books, and heard of in the accounts of others, but the real, accursed, living thing, experienced firsthand, as all truth is known.

God is the essence of immanence; the source of non-separation; the strings of String Theory; everything that gives rise to every thought, every sense, every intuition before it's had.

We attract our realities by the nature of our nature, such that within is always without, and such that perception parallels the truth.

Outrage = awareness = cynicism = true realism.

People build their entire lives around a fictionalized fantasy of God and the Everything, called religion, when all the while God, the Everything, is within everything, and every fiction is inked with the truth of God, and no truth may be superior to any other, and each is perfectly bespoke, called Gnosticism.

The destruction of the self is the revelation of the Self. To be the artist is to subdue the animal, such that its essence may be known. It's easy to tantalize the senses, or empower the body, with one's intake. The best food provides equal measures of both. Ambrosia.

Being of God, every animal possesses the same innate capacity for wisdom. It's all a matter of the extent to which their mind may capture it with worded circumscription, and the extent to which their wills may enact it.

The more subtle the communication, the more truth it carries, the more peace it provokes. The louder and more forceful it is, the greater its void of veracity, the more violent its enactment. Thus is truth as the hurricane, the perfect eternal peace of the center forever encircled by forceful falsity. And thus are the greatest liars those who put on the loudest, most elaborate shows, while those that speak the truth utter it like whispers, knowing that no compensation is necessary. Upon this same spectrum is the distance between God and Satan measured.

Doubt is the seed of truth, certainty is its illusion. If it may be applied to anything and everything, it's both vague and veracious, and near to the nature of absolute truth. If it can only be applied to something, it's constrained by specificity to definition and narrow application, nearing the definitiveness of the relative relationship between fact and fiction.

The salvation of humanity lies in atavism; in a reversion to, or rediscovery of, a natural, symbiotic relationship with the innately spiritual, medicinal realm that we've decimated with the parasitic pantheon of the seemingly perpetual pandemics of religion, materialism and the capitalistic degradation of a divinity that can only ever reciprocate our relationship with It. We cannot but receive what we give It; we cannot but make of ourselves what we make of It; we cannot but know God without knowing Its nature; we cannot but reap what we bid It to sow.

'Cultural appropriation' isn't immoral, it's history, society and global culture; this is but another example of the untruthful misleading of political correctness. Not only are we all intermixing all the time, and is every culture an 'appropriation' of countless others of which it came in intermixing past and present contact, but if you utilize an idea from 'another culture' in a respectful manner and with purity of intention, then you're actually *honoring* that culture. To purport that this is wrong because 'you're not from that culture' or 'you're just the dominant white race bastardizing it' is to perpetuate racism and discord, making you a part of the problem. If, for example, I study the use of entheogenic medicine (like Psilocybe cubensis) and use it in what's similar to what the Native Americans call a 'vision quest,' I'm honoring those naturalistic practices of spiritually connecting with myself and Mother Nature. This is a practice inherited from God and the Divine Mother, it isn't owned by any of Father or Mother's embodiments or tribes. Any Native American or anyone else that says that my entheogenic vision quests are wrong because I'm a 'white man' is the one committing the wrong, and is, ironically, blocking the inseparability ritual it stands for. We're all a part of the evolution of the One through the Infinite. Should I, as a Greek by blood, most identify with the Greeks, per prideful egotism? Should I say: You know what, most of western society was inherited from Greece through the Roman conquest through the evolution of Europe all the way to America, and you 'Americans' are unjustly 'culturally appropriating my culture' when you speak of a democracy that you don't actually possess (it didn't authentically exist in Ancient Greece either, but that's another story), or cite Hippocrates or Plato, or utilize Corinthian Columns, or do most anything in which 'my culture' is imbedded in this one? Honor 'your culture,' yes, but not to the extent where you believe it isolated and superior to everything constituting Culture.

The abuse of medicine is poison. Thus may the distance between the wise woman and the wicked witch be measured by dosage.

The truth is typically the opposite of what's said, even to oneself. For what's said is typically compensating the ego for what's true.

All of the most valuable resources, and the most potent people, are formed by the combination of two forces: pressure and time.

If you think that your 'net worth' is about money, you're a part of the problem.

True leaders are led by the One. They're only true leaders because they're being truly led.

All evidence is meaningful, but little of it means what we think it means at first. For all interpretation passes through fear and insecurity, phantoms turning fact to fiction.

We don't MAKE money, as though we produced it entirely within and of ourselves, detached from everything else. As with equating a person's worth with their wealth, as in the term 'net worth,' 'making' money is but veiled 'free market' propaganda, invisible to all but those who see through their indoctrination. For if you examine the full socioeconomic causality, the entire socioeconomic causal web, you'll find that money is more accurately EXTRACTED, mostly from the disadvantaged people and unprotected places of the planet. We just can't see the causal link between the cash we hold in hand and what it was derived from. Look closer and you'll find that equating wealth and self-worth unsustainably destroys people and planet, and that a revolution is coming, not just because it's right, but because it's necessary for the salvation of all.

Thoreau said: "The cost of anything is the amount of life that you exchange for it." The full, fundamental guiding principle may be stated as: "The cost of anything is the amount of life that you pay for it, while the value of anything is the amount of life you gain by it." Look close enough, and you'll find this lesson to be universally applicable.

God is the innermost Self common to all selves, the Devil is the outermost self common to one self. God is the ubiquitous interconnective spiritual tissue. The Devil is the isolated, divisive egotistic tissue. With every act, with every thought, you follow one or the other, and condition your responses to each, training to follow divinity or egotism.

Nearing your center is nearing God.

If you're always adding value to life whilst divesting from your ego, you're always right.

Conventional society is debilitating dependency and unsustainable sickness sold for profit. The only salvation is the filter, moving towards a naturalist lifestyle and removing all unnaturality sold to weakness.

Sometimes you have to empty yourself out before you can be refilled.

Strength is gained more by denying than by acceding; more by subtraction than addition.

The less pleasure you need from substances, the more substantive your pleasures will be.

***

The nature of the self is to be a conduit of the Self relative to the self; to receive and express the Self relative to the environment, experiences and capacities of the self.

'First, do no harm' is violated by every doctor with the writing of every unnecessary, dependency-producing prescription, and every failure to educate the patron towards 'food is medicine,' and away from the reliance upon profit-over-people conventional healthcare.

Spirit is the pure, irreducible, conscious spiritual energy of which everything is made. Nature is its inseparable embodiment. Spacetime and the matter made of Its relatively fixed condensation constitute the existential framework for immortal Spirit to exist as infinite finite, mortal beings. Nothing of Spirit is destroyed, only forever rearranged. Thus do I say that Spirit is Infinite of One, and that you're essentially divine.

'Development' is demise. What the prevailing realists, materialists and egotists sell as 'progress' is really dehumanization and denaturalization catalyzing either an atavist rebellion else humanity's eventual extinction. Mother Nature can only, by the inviolable laws of equal and opposite, equilibrium-seeking principle innate to Her, react in a

Self-defensive, parasite-purging manner. Returning to nature is salvation, following the 'development' of capitalism is ensuing doom.

Self-belief, self-love, is absolutely indispensable to happiness and success. But not the hollow, compensatory, egotistic form; not the type whose towers soar as high as its self-esteem sinks into the minimizing basement; rather, the true form of self-belief based upon Self-knowledge; the type that's hard-earned, not easily shaken, approaching the invulnerability of spiritual revelation, impervious to the inevitable attacks triggered by the worshipping of specifications of God.

It's all One thing of infinite variance, born from One into Infinite of One for the sake of endless variety. Genesis is what rendered you an indispensable element of divinity, the divine seed embodied through Mother Nature, She whom gives birth based upon the evolving conditions of Her holy form.

'Cult' and 'commune' are little more than words, almost exclusively used by dominant society to discredit groups and beliefs which threaten that dominance, so that non-critical thinkers will obediently dismiss them per their social conditioning. Don't forget that as soon as a system of beliefs attracts a following that refutes conventional societal standards (which are formed entirely for the sake of slaking and perpetuating greed), and that countering society decides to form its own community, you have a 'cult' that's become a 'commune.' True community, built around shared spiritual identity, is what the oppressing rulers have ALWAYS been most afraid of. That fear and defense of greed is the basis of both conservatism and religion.

The true evil witch isn't what the Church, in its need to suppress paganism and maintain power, programmed the people to believe that she is. She has nothing to do with herbalism, magic and belief in the divine nature of Mother Earth. The true, evil witch is what is made from a combination of innate cunning, moral underdevelopment and egotistic overdevelopment; a combination producing duplicity, deviousness and egotistic power trips, especially when she's sexually alluring, and the attraction grants her greater power. She's further empowered by a modern politically correct world wherein the Woke and Me Too movements enable her to manipulate her societal position in eliminating any threats to her power, including the women with whom she competes for social ranking and the attention of men, and any man she finds a threat.

Need exists in inverse proportion to freedom.

Just as only the brightest light may dispel the deepest darkness, so does it require those of the greatest good to effectively battle the greatest evil. And there's no way to make oneself the greatest champion of good without understanding the nature, motives and tactics of evil. So it is that those whom come to tame the lion must live in its den.

As we gaze upon the world, few of us see anything other than ourselves. For the ego is like a house of mirrors projecting self, reflected back at us in endless ways, and everywhere we turn we're bounced back. Only those most secure in and accepting of themselves can see *through* the looking glass.

Abusers, regardless of gender and other particularities, and regardless of outward appearance and the words they say and the egos they form, regardless of their presented extrinsic qualities, all have one thing in common: they feel small on the inside; they're intrinsically tiny. Thus, if we, as a society, wish to reduce abusiveness, we must treat the sense of smallness held by the abusers. This means granting more opportunity, support, purpose, sense of belonging and, ultimately, the love that leads them to the self-love, the inner fullness, which displaces the miniscule monster that abuses. For the problem is that we look upon the abusers simply as villains, caring only for their punishment, and caring not for what MAKES the monster. Like the evils of conventional healthcare, this is akin to treating the symptoms, not the cause. To treat the cause we must treat the societal deficiencies which lead the psychologically vulnerable to become the monsters, rather than simply punishing them after the people and potential they were are malformed into the monstrosity that their tininess produces. And the truth is that criminality and mental illness largely share the same causes, the same correlating sense of inner tininess and connected financial, social and psychological pressures, and that most of the causes of these issues, abusiveness, criminality and mental illness, can ultimately be traced to the failures of society to provide support, meaning, community, connection, purpose and opportunity whilst constantly applying pressures connected to classism, consumerism and egotism. The monsters, in other words, are created through a combination of psychological vulnerability and societal pressure, and the failure of divide and conquer capitalism to fill the cracks into which the vulnerable tumble, stewing in the toxins, becoming monsters.

We can't all be worker bees. Some of us are here to protect the worker bees; to question the queen and, if necessary, to help the workers rise up against her.

The solution to the unsustainable evils of divide, disempower and conquer capitalist society and its conservative culture is the semi-socialistic unite, empower and partner communal society that they've conditioned us to conflate with the communist regimes of the past. This is done for one reason only: to keep us economically weak and mentally unresisting of their ability to prey upon the disadvantages in us that they parasitically exacerbate and perpetuate. So, while the prevailing conservative paradigm has conditioned you to think of communities coming together in mutually supportive symbiotic development as 'communes' comprised of 'cult followers' the truth is that this is actually the communalism which offers salvation to an ever more divided, corroded, untenable humanity, and is the natural form of communal life endemic to all nativism.

If you don't love me it's because you don't really know me. The same can be said of everyone and everything. And there's the answer: full observation, listening until understanding becomes and breeds love.

'Dualism' means being deluded by the illusion of definite differentiation; it means being deceived by the appearance of absolute separation of things that as all being distinct things, obscuring the non-dualist truth that everything is but a facet of the One thing. Thus is dualism the basis for all misleading ideologies and value systems, including 'science is God' materialism and realism as well as the specious specificities of religion. Only the unitive knowledge of Spirit saves.

Human dignity moves in inverse commensuration with technological advancement, because the evolution of the machine is the devolution of the human. The innate, forgotten need to mentally advance and to spiritually connect to our fellow human beings and to Mother Nature who gave birth to us and harbors our existences has been superseded by artifice. Nature is being consumed by the machine both globally and within the human being. The more it thinks for us, and the more that we experience our lives through it, the more that reality is a fabrication, the more that essence is buried beneath perception. Today's youth is so void of integrity they think that 'honor' is a slogan for the Marines, that face to face communication is an archaic imposition, and that social media popularity and financial wealth are the measures of personal worth.

Don't look for role models, look for inspirations. For two reasons: (1) a role model is a version of idolatry, which is a version of egotism, which is the antithesis of truth, especially all-inclusive spiritual truth (and, ironically, is central to the error of 'one prophet' religion) (2) connected to the first point, you shouldn't be looking to 'play a role;' to fabricate yourself and imitate some perfect form and function. Rather, you should follow your heart and mind and realize that the everyone's authentic form is ever evolving, per the nature of the forever dynamic being that all of us always are.

It's the foremost objective of every insecure ego that spurs its small-feeling possessors to defend themselves against the existential threat of further self-reduction by attacking those people and ideas which they perceive as bigger and more secure. Most of the interpersonal injustices of the world have this one thing in common: the sense of smallness attacking the sense of largesse so as to make the big seem smaller for the sake of enlarging self-perception. Pay attention to human behavior and you'll find this to be the foremost force: insecure egotistic assaults. People attack what they feel threatened by. To be attacked by the status quo upholding majority is proof that you're a progressive.

Provocation is a precondition of progressivism. You can't wake anyone from the stultifying slumber of complacency without challenging their assumptions. But know that those locked into their cages will confuse your attempt to free them with the attempt to attack them, and, like caged, wild animals, they'll assault those that come to save them, biting and clawing, desperate to remain locked to the invisible enslavement that they call the one and only truth and reality. For that is what the Devil does: he locks you into invisible cages and convinces you to call the saving angels the demons.

We're *within* Consciousness. We're inside the Universal Mind. Spacetime and matter *are* energy. Energy *is* God. Everything is indivisible from the One thing. Nature is matter evolving to fit spacetime. Everyone has a prophet in their hearts, the entry point for Spirit into matter. These sentences are the same, and when you channel them as purely as possible, you embody 'The Christ.'

It's of the greatest possible irony that anyone who calls his or her self a 'Christian' could be offended by what I have to say. It's proof of the editorial censorship at the root of the intertwined history of tyranny and empire. It's like tearing trees from the forest to build a home in which you'll live, then pretending as though life has nothing to do with trees.

Don't believe the modern materialist or the religious pretense that you're separate from God. When you have a conversation with yourself in the absence of your small self, your ego, when you give internalized voice to the thoughts emerging from your innermost Self, you're speaking with indwelling divinity.

Let go of your need to label everything; to categorize and classify. That is your conditioning within materialist, capitalist society. Acknowledge and try to perceive and live and love through the deeper truth that distinctions are ultimately illusory, and that the purpose of the sense of separation is to allow for an infinite variety of the oneness.

I'm like Jerry Rice or Michael Jordan. You can't stop me. You can only hope to contain me. And even this is foolish, of course. For even if you kill this physical person, those forces which I've come to know and love more than myself cannot be killed, for they are the core of my Self, and shall always be there, and shall forever refill the most expansive containers into which they pour.

The perceiver is the perceived = God. It also = nothing is created or destroyed, Buddha, the double slit experiment and Schrodinger's Cat.

✴✴✴

All brilliant people are invariably faced with the question: could *I* be the Messiah? But unlike the way that the modern materialist, conservative, religious paradigm of mind-control wants you to believe that asking this question of yourself is an indication of your possession of a 'Messiah Complex' denoting mental illness and the need for dumbing-down, desensitizing, mind-numbing, denaturing, poisonous pharmaceutical intervention, what it usually means is that you intuitively sense your oneness with Consciousness (i.e. God, or Spirit) more than most. *It's actually an indication of spiritual intelligence, not mental illness.* Everyone has the capacity to connect with their innate sense of the perceived being the same as the perceiver. Some are just, by their natural mental gifts, and through certain practices (like meditation, fasting and psychonautics), more aware of their oneness than most. In fact, the more that this question persists, the more likely you are to end up at the conclusion that 'Messiah' is simply a term for the greatest possible relativity of awareness.

The most divine of all abilities is observation without self-projection. Listen. See. Sense. Presence: the sacred source of satiation.

Mushrooms are like combing the consciousness. The same discomfort required to untangle knots in the hair to straighten it out are experienced by the mind, the benefits of which are well worth the discomfort. We all get tangled up in the knots of ourselves.

It doesn't matter if it's new. Nothing is truly new. It's the ego that needs what we think and say to be considered novel and owned by us. It matters if it's *true*, and of value to life.

Yes, Hell is other people. The rub? So is Heaven. In fact, Heaven is God is *everyone*.

If you summon the strength to refuse the short term gratuitous pleasures, you're rewarded with the far superior long term pleasures of fulfillment. For the cost of accruing gratuity is the leaking of fulfillment.

There's no difference between work that you believe in and purpose, worship or freedom.

Anyone that needs proof that the ideology of evil is conservatism (i.e. dominating, conquering, materialist, egotist, small-minded, fear-based Christian culture) need look no further than *Wild, Wild Country* and what conservatism did to a true spiritual leader and his followers' attempt to establish a counter-cultural commune. I'm not saying that many heinous mistakes weren't made by Osho's followers, but any truly moral, open-minded, discerning viewer of that series will recognize that it was by and large the mentality and agenda of conservatism that pushed those followers to commit those mistakes. It's strongly reminiscent of 'The Domino Theory,' McCarthyism, the conflation of socialism with the tyranny of the egomaniacs that adopted and betrayed it, and the drug war and its persecution of any substance that expands the mind and naturally fosters resistance to capitalism and its egotism, greed, materialism and consumerism. Osho was on the right track, and make no mistake: the salvation of humanity lies upon a parallel track, and it's a *circular* track that's coming back around.

Hope is sanity. Expectation is disappointment.

Of all the underappreciated, undervalued, underdeveloped skills at humanity's disposal, the top 2 are: (1) breathing (2) listening.

You get out what you put in because output is an equal and opposite reaction to input.

'Misfit' is meant to be a pejorative term, but only a fearful, peer-pressured fool is so insecure and driven by the desire for acceptance and popularity that their need to fit in is greater than their need to stand out and become unbounded selves that can't be stuffed into 'fitting' prefabricated boxes.

To become one with the outermost, you must pass through the innermost. For the innermost is the source of the outermost.

The challenge for the moral and progressive human is to be able to acknowledge your indignation relative to the evil in the world whilst maintaining your gratitude for the wealth of love and experience also in that world. The challenge is to be able to be the activist indignant towards and battling the evil while not letting this sour you, the ill feeling balanced by gratefulness for the good.

The particulars disappear, but the Source from which they forever spring and respring never disappears, for It's eternal. Thus defines the difference between religion and spirituality, between cause and effect, between the lasting root and deciduous leaf.

Those that assume they're full cannot receive. The only way to be filled is to empty yourself. Only the Nothing can fit Everything.

One cannot know what others know by hearing it from those others. The others can only point the way to the realization, they cannot be the realization. I may point you to the eternal spring, but only you can drink, and cleanse yourself of the traditional mire.

The Whole is the absence of its parts.

After falsely dividing the people from God, the next step is dividing them from their work through the businesses constituting the economy. The equity holders being set at odds with the employees, the customers and the planet is the foundation of capitalism. Think about what a 'successful business' actually is. It's one person, or a select, excluding group of people, getting rich OFF OF its workers, its customers and the planet. Place dividing lines between these identities, and make sure most of the benefits go in one direction: to the equity holders. This movement can only come at the cost of everyone and everything else in the capitalist equation; it's the only way to equalize the equation, because a profit can never come from nowhere. Rather, a profit comes from everywhere BUT those who're profiting. Profit is a product of exploitation and extraction. And so long as this remains the basis of business and economics, business can never be moral, and economic activity can only unsustainably lead to growing disparities in all things of value, and to the destabilization of the planet. Until business and economics distribute their profits to all participants based upon the merit of their contribution, and until the protection of the planet supersedes extraction, evil results. And these are but the financial, material and ecological costs; this is BEFORE even considering the psychological and spiritual costs of denying community, commonality, collaboration, sharing, solidarity and the like that go along with it; the costs of denying our spiritual nature as united, communal beings.

To address a common mistake of both psychological treatment and some interpretations of Buddhism, let's be clear: Nothing is ever 'let go.' Nothing that is in us can ever be perfectly erased or extracted from us. Mental healing is never a surgical extraction. Rather, mental healing is about changing your perspective upon and making peace with your past, through an understanding of cause and the divestment in a limited, egotistic version of yourself as though it's who you absolutely are. If you're able to do this, the malignancy is made inert.

The ongoing irony for me in my interactions with those 'on the right' is that I'm fighting for them as much as any 'group of people,' but they're so perfectly brainwashed by

Christian dogma and conservative propaganda that they mistake me for the enemy while continuing to support those that keep them in their cages. The enemy is the one who raised you to exist in Plato's Cave, I'm the one standing outside of it, pointing a flashlight into it, trying to induce your exit.

If you really delve down into it, looking at the total health, moral, environmental and *spiritual* cost, you can do no other than realize that humanity's need for animal products is a CORE constituent in the evils we commit against ourselves, life and the planet.

Why's the onus on *me* to convince *you*? It's time to convince yourself. I know the way to the river, but you have to be the one to drink.

My heart belongs to God, and to those few who've come to inhabit it, becoming my personal divinities. And I'm certain of this even when the Devil comes to cage my consciousness and corrupt my corporeality.

Faith doesn't belong to the religious. In fact, the 'pagans' got there first, and have never left the innermost sanctum. We have a natural resistance to the unholy crusades.

The person that puts up the boundary is the one with the power. It's as much about possession as it is about protection. It all depends upon whether you're inside the boundary, or outside the boundary.

Not asking permission to tell the truth, either from ourselves, others, or the enforcers, is called *honor*. Asking is called *cowardice*.

Undefinable. noun. That which is, or those that are, unable to be boxed.

One possible interpretation of the double slit experiment says that reality is produced relative to awareness. That is, something only is, only exists, when we're giving it our attention; when we believe that it exists. Otherwise it remains the potential for existence; the energy awaiting you to literally make it matter. Like *The Matrix*: there is no spoon until you believe there's a spoon. The spoon bends around you. Paying witness manifests the witnessed. Thus do you contribute to Consciousness relative to your awareness of It. The subjects collectively conceive the shared objects out of themselves; out of universally shared Spirit, the pure conscious source of creation.

No one can be pulled across the threshold separating ignorance from knowledge. You can only be shown the door by those that've already opened and passed through it.

Don't ask: what will make me the most popular? Ask: how may I most be of service? Providing the most valuable possible service of yourself will produce an authentic popularity, as the greatest popularity that a person may possess parallels their purpose.

We're all trying to earn our freedom from the secret soft enslavers, regardless of the extent to which we know that secret.

Your external environment is a product of your internal environment. The deepest, innermost part of you is the same as Genesis; it generates your reality relative to everyone else's genesis. So it is that what you think and how you feel is what you sense of the reality you're always in the process of creating. It's a perpetual feedback loop of belief and confirmation. You're constantly turning yourself inside-out, your intrinsic relationship with your consciousness creating your relationship with The Consciousness collectively constituting reality. This doesn't mean that physical laws don't exist, it means that they're subject to metaphysical force.

Levels of knowing are levels of perception. An incomplete perceiver cannot completely possess his/her perception, because he/she is as a vessel with holes. Such a vessel cannot contain its perception. As you fill yourself with Self-awareness, with Self-knowledge, you're as a more solid, better-containing vessel. You may fill yourself more, and pour more of yourself to slake the thirst of others, in service to life; for service of life is service of God, as God manifests through nature as life.

Words themselves are dead, passing from mind to mind only, inert, void of vitality. Their value isn't in themselves, as they possess no living truth. Their value lies in their ability to construct the signs pointing the mind to where the vital truth lives within the heart, take it into itself, and gain its livening force.

Ironically, materialist, realist society has denatured and dishonored all material things, denying the divinity extant within all things, thus concealing the truest indwelling reality.

Black and white dichotomies are the illusory makings of misleading absolutes. Something is experienced as 'bad' in the moment, when time is relatively fixed. But when a 'bad' ultimately begets a good, time shows that the 'bad' never was; the momentary 'bad' was the causal cost of the good. The good simply needed time to grow from the bad. Thus must we have faith in ultimate causality. We must have faith that what is 'bad' summons the good; that evil accidentally serves good by being its catalyst. So it is that suffering never exists in a vacuum, and that all pain is actually a growing pain.

Needing credit for something reduces its authenticity and value. Truth is falsified when it needs to be recognized. The very act of looking for recognition reduces it, because authentic truth doesn't dress up or need to be seen. As soon as you try to gain recognition for truth, to sell it, it becomes a commodity and extension of the ego, thereby becoming less true. For ego and truth, like ego and love, are opposing forces. They cancel one another out. As with love, which is a form of truth, when the truth is legitimate, when it's most real, it's naked and natural; it's self-evident; it's substance sans show. For every show is a performance to conceal a lack of substance, the golden facades concealing the rotten interiors inhabited by emperors of ego overlorded by the shadow of themselves.

If you're *trying* to do something you've already failed to do it.

***

Discipline is the difference between knowing what to do and doing it. And what could be more valuable than closing the gap between *should* and *did*?

***

A 'mystic' is simply someone who operates based upon their innermost intuition, sensing all is in reflection of immanence. They sense, even if they don't know it intellectually, that their hearts are more than standalone sense, but are gateways to Spirit, the indwelling One of which everything is composed. The idealist is the intellectual counterpart to the mystic. In contrast with the 'realist' and materialist dominating the modern day mentality, their minds seek the knowledge of their hearts: that existence is a product of consciousness, rather than consciousness being a product of existence (of strictly biochemical, material, mechanistic interactions void of Spirit).

The greatest irony of modern human existence is that the Holy Ghost, Spirit, the subtlest of everything composing everything, the indwelling, universal Self, is most real, whereas the observable phenomenon, the scientific of the realist and materialist, is the least real. Materialism is the observable flux subjective to yourself. Spirituality is the inwardly sensed absolute, the subject of every self. So it is that the forever fluctuating observable is called the real, the changeless absolute feeding fluctuation is called fantasy.

Every form of the mental belief in separation is a self-reduction. By falsely dividing you from Self through language, labels, classifications, categorizations, designations and the like, by believing that these artifices represent absolute truths, you're falsely divided from the innermost truth of non-separation, or non-duality. And the way in which humanity is subdued has always been through this tactic of divide and conquer. With every believed divide we become smaller, and weaker, and easier to control by the parasites that feed from the conquered.

The nearer that you draw to your essential nature the closer you come to enlightenment. For enlightenment is your truest nature; your most natural Self. Whereas individualized selfhood is the illusion; an illusion born of One becoming Infinite of One through the conversion of eternal energy into spacetime and matter; the endless rebirth of the Self into forms of Itself for the sake of variety. You're a self only relative to Self, subject subsuming object. It's the same as Saint-Expurey saying: "Perfection is achieved not when there's nothing left to be added, but nothing left to be taken away," and also his saying: "Here is my secret; a very simple secret: it is only with the heart that one can see rightly; what is essential is invisible to the eye." Heart is the third eye: the sight of the oneness beneath multiplicity.

Thoughts fill the void into which the truth thence cannot come. For truth, like love, rushes in to fill a vacuum. Without the vacuum the force that pulls it in is weak, and there's not enough room for it to fully fit.

Wisdom is found less through thought than through holding the mind in abeyance. Suspend your thought. Make your mind as a perfectly welcoming host. But don't trap your visitors inside. Let your thoughts pass through without being retained. If you clasp onto them, if you hold them inside, there won't be room to host the holiest guest.

'Lease' is synonymous with slavery. The lessee is the slave, the lease-holder is the slaveholder. One gets rich by denying ownership to the other, and keeping the lessee weak. The lease contract highlights the fact that slavery never ended, it just evolved. Capitalism didn't destroy the chains, it made them invisible to all but a few of us, most 'free people' wearing them without even knowing that they're there. The 'land of the free' is the land of those most enslaved by chains that they've been trained not to see, conditioned to call everything that might lead them to unbind themselves 'socialism,' and every link in their chain a facet of 'reality.'

A crime against anyone is a crime against The Self is a crime against yourself. For by the essential law of indivisibility, nothing done to anyone is divisible from anyone else. What is done by you is done to you. "What you do to the least of my brothers you do to me," Jesus said. As with all authentic sages he was operating from the ultimate illumination of non-separation. The Spiritual Rule says what The Golden Rule should've said: Do unto others as you'd have done unto yourself, for there's essentially no difference.

Awareness is purer than thought. Thoughts occlude the lens through which the light of consciousness passes. Knowledge is purity of experience upon which our words piggyback.

Look with empty eyes. Look without self-projection. Only without projecting yourself will you truly see. When we project ourselves, when we observe with ideas and labels and preconceptions about the world and ourselves we see our self-reflection. Only when we see without consciousness may we see with Consciousness. Only free from self-projection do we see the Self-reflection.

Some that're labeled insane are near to enlightenment, for they live within a reality independent of the illusion of 'one reality.' Most of what's called true is near conformity, 'truth' constituted by popular confirmation.

Like the newborn, the sage assumes nothing.
You can only see infinite possibility by not
imposing a limited possibility upon your sight.

Many ones have known The One.

I'm one of them.

You mind is the antenna.

Your heart is the broadcast.

The endpoint of intelligence is to abandon intelligence; is to transmute the egotistic need to be smart into raw awareness. I only know because I don't know. I only know it because I don't think that I know it. I know the truth when I don't try to define and box it in. As soon as I call it something, as soon as I try to box it into something in which it'll never fit, the box collapses. This book is one of my boxes, and it only contains what the reader can see not in, but *through* the words.

Stop defining. Truth, like God, is non-definition; the absolute center.

Truth is the merging of object and subject.

Psychologically, we all live in haunted houses. We're all haunted by the traumas, pains and privations of our pasts. But running from them only makes you more afraid of them, and commensurately empowers them. And trying to dispel them, and exorcise them from your dwelling, doesn't work, because it's a form of focusing on and empowering them. Instead, simply acknowledge their existence when they come, then let them pass. Don't purposefully summon them, and don't further empower them by focusing on them, making them more real. Let them come and go without strengthening them with your thoughts, and they'll fade. In the meantime, focus on the things you want in your home, summoning the spirits of manifestation to displace the haunting phantoms with the materializing of that made relative to belief.

***

Political correctness is the glorification of self-righteous bullying, censorship and conformity.

***

The more popular you are, the less likely you are to speak your heart and mind, for two reasons: (1) popularity is generally garnered not by challenging people, not by going against the popular belief system and telling people what they need to hear, but by confirming that belief system and telling people what they want to hear (2) the popular have too much to lose; too much of a disincentive to tell people anything that goes against popular opinion and thereby risks the money, power and social standing of the popular person (the political effect).

Reality is a competition of consciousness built by belief. We prevail not when we're the most rationally correct, but when our convictions are greater than those of our competitors. We prevail when our belief is greater than doubt; our own doubt, and the doubt of those whose beliefs conflict with our own. And overcoming our own doubt is the critical first step. For when we truly believe, and when we manifest our reality relative to our beliefs, others can't help but take notice. For true belief is contagious, and its procreative power is its own persuasion. Thus, even when we're conditioned to believe something else, in the face of a true believer we begin to believe what they do. And from this sharing of belief may the force for change mount, and may we shuck off the age-old yokes, and remake our shared reality.

Enlightenment is observation without self-projection; the spiritual Self freed from self-confirmation; the universal Mind sans the ego enforcing itself upon the mind. When we see from the ego we impose its delusions upon the world and call it sanity. This is the looking glass of common sight. When the few see without wearing the egotistic glasses, imposing nothing upon the world, seeing only what's truly there, we call it insanity. This is the uncommon sight of seeing through the looking glass at the ubiquity of divinity.

God grows in the gaps between our thoughts. The greater the gap between your thoughts, the more that Mind may dwell within your mind, the more the self is set aside, the nearer you come to the universal Self.

Suffering breeds sagacity. For experience is the only true teacher, and only through the absence of anything may we know its value, indelibly stamped into us through the suffering of its deprivation.

Distillation is the alchemy of the philosopher; to transmute the infinitely complex many into the clarity of the ever fewer, until finally reducing it all into the certainty of the One.

What greater irony than the consummate rebel against unjust imperial authority being converted by Empire into the consummate symbol of conformity? What greater irony than those whom say they follow the representative of God following the deceivers? What greater proof of the power of propaganda than the darkness consuming and pretending to be the light, the blinded walking in the dark pretending to be the sighted? Those that claim to follow the words of the rebel are now conservatives conserving the power of his enemies; the perfect hypocrites, they conserve the traditions of greed and ego which he fought. They say that the greatest trick of the Devil is convincing the world that he doesn't exist. I disagree. The greatest trick of the Devil is convincing the world that he speaks for God.

The result of too much practicality is an obscurement of vision, a loss of imagination, an absence of belief and a forsaking of meaning. The practical do well financially in a world in which romantic, spiritual and creative impracticalities are seen as costly distractions, and yet, to the impractical, the costs of forsaking them is far greater. No amount of money or social acceptance, the surface of success, can compensate or pay for the wealth buried beneath practicality.

One of the greatest problems with the dominant modern drive towards professional specialization is that wisdom is always *general* in application. The specialist tends to be too myopic to see the widest ranging, wisest truths. In fact, the more universal the application of any truth, the truer it is, the more wisdom it contains, the closer it is to *philosophy* - in the Greek, literally meaning "love of wisdom." Whereas if it's only true esoterically, within a specific field, for a specific group of people, it isn't *essentially* true, and the value of its application is minimal. Religion is the theological version of specialization; non-religious spirituality is the generalization.

Being successful in life isn't the same as being financially successful. And all those that're unsuccessful in life, even if they're financially successful, have one thing in common: the voices of others resound more loudly within them than does their own voice. If you don't listen to yourself, if you can't hear yourself over the din of others, you cannot become yourself, and no person that lives as anything other than themselves can be successful.

'Other' is the illusion. 'Other' is the ego, and the cause of all greed and evil. For when we awaken to the universally-shared Self, and the self dissolves into the Self, we know no 'other,' only forms of our Self. And so we cannot greedily hoard, for we take from our Self. And we cannot harm 'another,' only our Self. We are only a relatively separated self;

not an 'individual self,' but an individualization of Self. So it is that the salvation of humanity lies in the awakening to Self, and the dissolution of illusive otherness.

You shall denounce the prophets as demons, for the true demons wear your priestly robes and pretend sainthood, and the Devil of Ego whom has made you believe that you're divided from divinity, from the spiritual Self, rules over you by falsified division. The Devil of Ego has claimed and twisted the lessons of the prophets to deepen your corruptibility and separate you from God and your brethren in your mind, even as this is but the core deception: you cannot be divided from your essential spiritual nature, regardless of your mind having been deceived. And the reawakening shall come when you remember that division is an illusion made to conquer, and that separation of body isn't separation of being, and that God dwells in *everything*.

The ambition of most of those raised in and indoctrinated into capitalist society is to become a slaveholder. It's never called that, of course, per the purpose and deceiving power of propaganda. But that's what the minority excluding ownership class *actually* is: the modern slaveholders using misleading words and ideas to conceal contemporary soft slavery. My ambition is different; it's of the few true moral human beings: to be an emancipator. And there can be no emancipation until the majority realize that they are slaves; enslaved in mind, in belief, and economically, and financially, and politically. The Devil is the God of Greed and Ego, and the ownership class are his demons. Let go of your demonic possession; release your ambition to become one of his minions.

No man is apart. All man is a part.

As an absolute end death is an illusion. It's only the finite forms that end, never the forever enduring function of form.

***

Christ is the eternal part of every person; the infinite and formless forever reforming every finite form. Every person is endowed with the prophet, but must dig down as deeply into themselves as possible to summon him/her.

Divinity is the capacity to find the center.

Our relative separation is accentuated by the aristocratic masters, taught as absolute so that our sense of separation could be taken advantage of. And through this Original Sin committed by the Church were we divided. And through this division are we weak. And through this weakness are we conquered. And, being conquered, we are the debilitated host, unable to shed the leeches latched onto it, feeding off of humanity. This is human history as handed from Rome to Europe to Church and State to Western Capitalism.

If I come into the discourse in the spirit of brotherhood, and you come into the conversation to beat me, I already won.

Awareness of otherness is relativity of wrong.

***

You either believe that reality is within the box or that reality is outside the box. And trust me, the box can't contain reality.

You can't connect people on the level of the mind. Not truly. None can know another on that level, because every mind and experience of existence is unique, and there's therefore no way for any mind to completely understand another mind, such that empathy is always imperfect. You have to connect people on the level of the heart. Because the force that animates and dwells within every heart is the same, and, therefore, the only knowledge of another is through their heart, finding that knowledge of them is knowledge of yourself, the spiritual revelation of non-duality; the infinite bridge between the One.

Economically, the only thing that's valued is the commodity that's in demand, and that's far more about product salesmanship than product quality. For example, out of 1,000 intelligent writers, all with valuable things to say, the one that's valued isn't the most intelligent writer or even the best writer, but the one that successfully sells himself; the one in a thousand that successfully convinces himself and others that he's worth reading. Else he's unread. And it starts with convincing yourself; with selling yourself to yourself. Because if you're not convinced of yourself, you won't be able to convince others of yourself, because they'll sense that you don't have confidence in what you're selling, and it won't sell, regardless of its inherent value.

As Rumi said: "Everything in the universe is within you." The same force of pure conscious generative energy that big banged from Oneness into Infinite of One ('God' or 'Spirit') is within you. It's the essential-most, irreducible constituent of everything and everyone. And we will our realities from this same divine force. Science accidentally says the same thing, it just doesn't understand the spiritual implications, and arrogantly attempts to divide material from source. But all form begins with formless energy being harnessed to form a function. The "nothing is ever created or destroyed, only forever rearranged" of physics is really saying: "nothing comes from nothing, and nothing can become nothing; zero only exists in math, for the sake of balancing equations; we're all an inseparable part of the constant reproduction of the same eternal, fundamental force of pure energy." Einstein's "curved space theory" states that "energy tells spacetime how to curve, and curved spacetime tells matter how to move." And like spacetime bending around energy, we bend reality to fit our wills. We physically enact this bend, but it begins with the pure force of conscious will within us. We decide something is going to be real, and we make it real. The material universe is simply the enaction of One divine will through infinity.

Meditation is the practice of producing gaps of thought into which God may enter; of generating gaps in consciousness which Consciousness may enter. When the consciousness and self are active, the Consciousness and Self cannot be heard. But with practice the gaps can grow, and the silent stillness may be deepened. So it is that through meditation one may develop nearness with the One, and eventually develop the ability to set the ego (the small self) aside for extended periods, and observe their own consciousness from the perfectly equanimous Consciousness (the big Self).

We're separated so that we may come together. We're lost so that we may be found through others, and thereby discard our division, and render otherness obsolete, the fractures healed and reformed into One.

There's an innermost essence, a truest nature, at the core of every endowment of Consciousness. Around this pure energy of being matter condensed into identity, and spacetime spawned relative separation. So it is that our innermost oneness, God, expanded the indistinct forms of the One divine body. And from this the Devil spawned from the power that may be taken by focusing on and broadening distinctions. The Devil's deception is to make you forget your innermost spiritual nature as an extension of God; to make you believe you're a distinct, divided body; that you're one separate entity, or 'soul,' that must go one way or the other in the afterlife (all divided dichotomies are oversimplified falsities) else is fated to be endlessly reincarnated until it egotistically escapes the bondages of selfhood. Thus separated in your mind you're already amenable to the divide and conquer that the Devil uses to slake the demons of greed and ego, blind to the emancipating truth of non-division being the foundational base of being.

Too much practicality murders creativity and becomes an inhibiting, prohibitive force.

Let me tell you why the epitome of egomania putting on the big boy pants and playing president in the parade is accidentally a good thing for America: it pacifies the hair-trigger simpletons whilst galvanizing the progressive intellectuals. Chump's election thus simultaneously keeps the tenuous peace whilst laying the groundwork for revolution. His referring to himself as 'The Chosen One' is also comically perfect, as all demonic demagogues do this: demons dress in the attire of the Messiah that Empire hijacked.

***

MAGA: Manipulate American Gullibility Again

***

What do I *want*? I want whatever you're willing to give in exchange for whatever I'm willing to give, and I definitely don't just mean money. Is that not the purpose of every interaction between every form of the One?

***

Just keep pulling on the collective consciousness until it begins bending in your direction. Don't worry about *what* (who) you're pulling on and why it's (they're) so resistant to bending. Just keep pulling, bending otherness towards your self-belief.

The truth is invisible. That's something the scientists and materialists and egotists and realists will never understand: the essence of reality is immeasurable. This general demographic possesses low spiritual intelligence; poorly developed intuition. They have to be hit over the head with Thor's Hammer before they realize that Thor exists.

Most human interactions are on the level of ego; of perceived separateness; the shadow play dancing over the truth. Only when we see and connect with our hearts are we interacting upon the ground, intertangled with the roots beneath the surface.

※※※

'Conservative:' synonym for 'mark.'

'Cynic:' synonym for 'aware.'

※※※

Truth follows perception.

※※※

The truly spiritual (not the religious) are never in jeopardy. Regardless of what happens to their physical person they know that what's most true of them, their innermost essence, can't be killed. Due to this highest faith they possess a peace that can't be touched by those forever feeling in jeopardy, including those deluded into believing that they have a separated soul that's in jeopardy of eternal damnation, or that's slated to stay stuck in reincarnation.

The point of material is dynamism.

It's easier to measure than to know.

***

Know the truth of yourself through your pain.
If you know only pleasure, and use it to
conceal the pain, you're hiding from truth.

***

Knowledge is the shadow cast by truth.

***

Solipsism times = Truth.

Both the body and mind make incessant noise. And yet you only hear the truth when they're quiet.

You're a drop in your own ocean; a leaf sprouting from your own tree, blowing in the winds of eternity.

In the end the most important question will be: How much life did I live? In other words: How many moments rich with love, fun and purpose was I fully steeped in?

Don't force your teachings upon others, wait for them to ask. For without asking there can be no reception, and without reception there can be no absorption, and without absorption nothing is taught. So it is that all learning must follow asking, and teaching is a vessel pouring into an open or closed vessel.

In the long bending arc of causality, everything is good, because everything is necessary. By the forces of destiny did I choose my own position relative to the material bend of my own spacetime.

You can't simultaneously pursue truth and popularity, because political incorrectness is often true and, by definition, unpopular.

Success runs relative to self-belief. It's about defining yourself rather than allowing yourself to be defined by others. It's about crafting your own role in life, based upon your convictions and sense of calling and purpose, rather than allowing yourself to be stuffed into boxes constructed and filled, and bought and sold, by others. It's about respecting your own opinion at least as much as anyone else's, so that you think and act without dependency upon others, shortening the bridge between you and success.

For a long time I've been aware of ego as being the nemesis of the spiritual philosopher. I've thought of the ego like an illusion or mirage; an unreal self-conception; like the shadow you cast against reality, the sun being your true self. Recently I've come to believe that it's not that the self you conceive is fake or unreal so much as fabricated. There is, in other words, a difference between ego and *identity*. Rather than an immaterial shadow or mirage, your identity is more like a tool that you craft in order to build the future you want, without which you live as the shadow. You arguably need the identity in order to be successful; in order to inspire others to believe in you. Because people need to see and be able to identify with those and that which and whom they believe in, and they can't do that with a shadow. You just have to realize that the identity that you craft is an impermanent fabrication utilized for temporal and terrestrial purposes, not the truest you. Harness identity, disregard ego and know that, in your core, you'll inevitably jettison both ego and identity and return to Source.

Only a truly self-secure person wants others to succeed, regardless of what they say. This is simply because others succeeding reminds the insecure person of their own relative lack of success, and thereby threatens their self-image. You have to have conquered yourself in order to truly wish well for others; i.e. your sense of self cannot be based upon others.

Everything is borrowed. Nothing is owned.

Capitalism means those who own the capital capitalize upon it by exploiting everyone and everything that doesn't own the capital. That's definitely *not* the best that we can do.

The more aware you are, the more disturbed you are by the human world, the more activism you develop.

Investing in the stock market is the same as investing in the ability of publicly traded companies to exploit the disadvantages of the people and the planet, which is the same as unsustainably broadening the disparity in all things of value possessed by the people and places of the planet, which is the same as supporting suffering and evil. Want to do something with your money? Invest in people, products and services which do the opposite of the stock market: improve the opportunities and quality of life of the underserved, under-protected people and places of the planet currently denied equity.

The only difference between absorbing nonsense and absorbing truth is the filter. Modernity erodes the filter, inundating you in nonsense. Philosophy is making the filter, which is why it's so undervalued by, and of the greatest potential value to, modernity.

I see the goddess in the woman that capitalism has prostituted. Let us remember our divinity divine brothers and sisters!

The battle is within. The without is mostly a projection of the within. Humanity is collectively producing its reality, carrying it forward as a type of composite self-projection. That projection is collectively produced, always progressing, and never, ever fixed as 'the one reality,' regardless of what the realists and materialists say.

It's all about the heart. The mind, for all of its apparent might, mostly just gets in the way of the truth and everything that gives life its innate value. In the end, it's all about the greatest of cliches: *listen to your heart*.

I shall be the River, where all that you've known before is the dam. Behold the glory of true love, that which drops to the lowest places from the highest places, and fertilizes every inch of the shared Self-manifestation.

You forever look out from yourself. So the question that most matters: what is *yourself*?

In a world of endless sensory overload and information inundation, of constant confusion and doubt, the simple, stressed mind has little means to keep from reaching for the comfort of false absolutes. Hence the appeal of the blowhard proclaiming that everything he does is 'the best.' We all reach for and cling onto those things that comfort and give our lives a sense of truth, clarity, meaning and purpose. But for those with highly limited mental faculties, this tendency leaves them open to grasping onto delusions that they believe ends their doubt, and thus leaves them highly vulnerable to those that well sell such false absolutes, lending the desperately needed illusion of total certainty.

There's an immeasurable evolution of collective consciousness, or Consciousness, at the heart of existence. Every individualized consciousness is an inseparable constituent of this collective evolution, and all that which is most essential to that evolution remains beyond every delusional human pretense of power. The Tao heeds not the human ideas of wealth and control born of the ego, but uses such illusions in the gradual revelation of the grounding truth underlying all of them, The Way walked by all. Those whom heed the shadows cast across the ground are captured by a world of illusion; a world that blinds them to the truth that they're but playing a shadow game set to serve The Way. For no matter how long humankind may ignore the eternal ground upon which it walks and dishonor its natural manifestations and divine guidance, the truth of It cannot be forever forsaken, for everything which seems to prevail over It yet depends upon It, and everything comes from and returns to The Way, like endless rivers running eternally back to the sea, to be rained once more. The unwise carve rivers and capture water in corralling dams for the sake of expanding their egos, proclaiming themselves masters of a new domain. The wise are as undammed rivers connecting and fertilizing life in its inseparability, forever riding those rivers back to the collective Source that'll forever be.

The words of the sages always mirror one another, for though the form peering into the mirror forever changes, every form is formed from the forever formless, and the mirror itself is unchanging and eternal. Thus is the formless reflected through infinite form.

Rather than forever filling space, practice holding space. Only then shall It enter.

Nothing true is forced. To be natural means to arise of its own volition, and come into itself without effort. The only other way is artifice. Thus the difference between the timelessness of truth arising in endless natural forms of Itself and the forever forced artifices of the human ego pressed into artificial forms for the sake of selling self.

The highest function of the mind is to 'hold the bridge' between itself and the heart; to free the mind of the intruding thoughts of the self, the intellect, ego and psyche, which block the bridge between the self and the Self; between the individualized consciousness and Consciousness.

The truth emanates from the exact center. The further you move away from it, the further away it moves from you.

The greatest effort is to make no effort. The greatest truth arises by not being sought. Completion is known by not moving away from yourself. Fullness can only fit within the perfectly vacant vessel.

You don't *create* enlightenment, you *remember* it, the consciousness awakening to Consciousness. You don't build it, you wipe away everything learned and identified that conceals it. *It's always been there*. It's the unchanging, ceaseless Self through which every form and idea of self ceaselessly passes and reforms. It's the changelessness in which all change occurs. It's the sky through which every cloud passes. The sun arcs across it, then the moon; it is bright, it is dark, it is cloudy, it is clear, but the sky itself is always there, unchanged, simply receiving the endless variety of forever changing form and phenomena which it hosts. It is never these things, it is that in which these things occur. The truest identity isn't the change, but the changelessness; the permanence forever hosting impermanence.

Observe the thought without being the thought. Thoughts are occurrences, not identities.

***

Honor and conviction are drifting towards extinction. Ever rarer is the person compelled by true belief, having developed an ideological foundation not made by others and possessing the courage and integrity to say what they think, even when unpopular.

***

The great mystery is that completion is achieved through separation; unification is formed from division; revelation is the light piercing the darkness; duality drives us back to our non-dualist nature; the Yin only need exist relative to its equally-opposite Yang.

Dividing anything from its source makes it unnatural, ineffective and evil in outcome. This is true of pharmaceuticals dividing nature from medicine, of religion dividing God from humanity, and sexuality from spirituality, of capitalism dividing people from ownership of their work and their homes, and of modern fake democracy passing votes through partisan filters, dividing the people from a direct say in their governance. Justice demands reconnecting people to nature, divinity, sexuality, business, politics and everything else, else the evil continues.

All people are self-serving. That's not 'selfishness,' it's simply the nature of being a self. The only question is whether or not you can serve one another simultaneous with serving yourself. And despite the rulers oppressing the people through divide and conquer, the answer is always: YES YOU CAN.

Every movie tells the same story: everything is a lie except that which comes from the heart. And yet the world is ruled by the lies, and ignores the heart. We tell ourselves the same story over and over, without heeding that story; without ever hearing ourselves.

God can't eradicate your doubt for you. God eradicates doubt through your own free will.

The innermost is the outermost. That which is most reducibly complex is composed of the irreducibly most simple. That which is as emptiness expands to become the completion. So it is that nearest to Source is the mage who facilitates the formation of fate from the faith of One. For from the eternal seed so small as to be invisible sprouts everything in existence, and those that cultivate It grow the truth. They but allow The Way to take its course. They coax what must be into reality. Necessity, fate, faith, causality and truth are One; the One forever expanding into the Infinite before returning to Itself, knowing Itself by becoming Infinite forms of Itself before returning to its perfectly protean potential.

Reality is built by belief, so much so that belief becomes fate. The problem with thinking, and with the perception of right and wrong and truth and ignorance, is that it's based upon doubt. Thinking is about filling perceived gaps in our knowledge. The intellect thus feeds upon doubts, and those doubts define the reality of the thinker. But the truth is that what becomes the reality of every person and the whole of humanity is that which is most purely believed, regardless of right and wrong, truth and ignorance. We fix our minds on the perception of absolute truths that don't exist, as the Source of our beings may become anything that we will It to be, such that all falsely fixed truths forever fluctuate and reform around what we most believe to be true. Purity of faith, faith in the innermost force, is taking the generative force in hand so as to build by belief.

Sink all the way into your innermost Self, that central stage in which Consciousness plays, and there reset your stage to produce the play that you want to see.

Sometimes you have to get lost swimming across seemingly endless seas of doubt before you can make landfall in the manifesting of belief. And the greater that which you believe, the more you have to stretch that belief across the seas in order to materialize it as the land upon which you'll stand.

***

Belief and doubt are the Yin and Yang of creation. The one always exists relative to the other, with reality born in the balance. Where there's a void in the one, the other always naturally rushes in to fill it. And the truth is always thus born in the battle for the space, that which settles into reality always being a product of the relativity of belief and doubt. Yet, there's another way: the opening up to the pure generative force through the dispossession of both. Rather than doubting or believing and making the manifestations of the conscious mind, one may divest of both and be borne along by the current of blind fate, neither paddling with nor against the tide. Thus may God makes us of Its pure will.

The closer to the center, the broader and more universal the application, the nearer to truth and God the thought or idea. If it's only true for a few, it's mostly a fabrication. If it's true for everyone, it's of the nature of God which births through the Mother at the conjunction of the axes of materialism and immaterialism; of the fixed and finite and the forever foundation forming from formlessness.

Rather than reaching for what you want, create the receptive conditions within yourself into which what you want is caught by the natural gravitational pull of creation. This is 'the secret;' the Law of Manifestation. Make the space within for it to fit, and the seed of it will plant itself in you, and it will grow to fill the space that was opened for it.

Vital force is gained by our nearness to necessity. Dissipation is caused by acting on the unnecessary.

The inner becomes the outer.

The further you go within, the further you go without.

Emily the Criminal

(In Response to the Netflix Film)

"Motherfuckers will just keep taking from you and taking from you until you make the goddamm rules yourself! Am I wrong?"

No Emily, you hit the nail on the head.

The holders of equity capitalize on that capital by exploiting the disadvantages of every non-equity-holder, including the planet itself. That's all capitalism really is: the crime of legalized theft. And the result is inevitable: criminals like Emily.

Capitalism creates cutthroat competitors compelled towards criminality, whereas our nature as social, spiritual beings is to be collaborators. Rather than working together towards mutually beneficial aims, those that own the capital pit us as competitors working against one another for their benefit. The cutthroat competition on the side of the non-equity-possessing workers creates economic pressures pushing us towards criminality in the fight for survival, then basic comforts and opportunities. And the corruptive aspect of wealth, power and greed on the side of the equity-possessors creates psychological pressures pushing them towards criminality in compelling the possession of ever more. So the result of capitalism is a complete dishonoring of the social and spiritual nature of human beings, compelling the unnatural, degradative economic atmosphere of cutthroat competition, pressure and criminality on all sides. The equity possessors are psychologically corrupted, and become consumed with exploiting the workers, buyers and the planet in the extraction of ever more wealth and power, and the non-equity-possessors are economically pressured, becoming consumed with overcoming the stresses of survival and the garnering of comfort and opportunities. The result is perpetual economic warfare, with the few feeding off of people and planet, all of which creates a broader unsustainable financial, sociological and environmental pressure in which humanity tears itself apart whilst ushering in planetary upheaval and our own inevitable demise. Thus it is that capitalism, especially when not balanced by the semi-socialistic principles of planetary protection and the sharing of equity, inevitably oppresses not just the quality of the collective lives of the human race, but dishonors our very nature, turning natural collaborators of a shared spiritual identity and brotherhood into the continued degradations of cutthroat competitors, criminals and whores selling our natures for greed. And the sadly ironic, humorous part of it all is that almost everyone is under the delusion that this is simply the way it is; as if this capitalistic construct is the very nature of human existence. Not only is this most definitely NOT the case, but this artificially contrived economic basis for existence (itself evolved through the history of Empire as a form of concealed, soft enslavement of the masses) is, as mentioned, entirely against the nature of humanity. It isn't the nature of humanity to exploit the weakness of others, as we're taught via the lie (embedded in the prevalent paradigm of 'realism' and 'materialism,' and in the lies of religion) of "that's just human nature." We have to be *taught* that this is the way. Our true nature is to work to reinforce one another and honor the planet, Mother Nature. This 'one reality' of dishonorable capitalism was taught to us for one reason: the greed of those whom have always taken advantage of disadvantage, from slavery to feudalism to capitalism, through the history of Empire.

Freedom exists relative to self-awareness. When you're thinking about yourself, when the self is in mind, you're in chains. When you're not in your own mind, when there's no self in mind, you're free.

Work without will is slavery. Will without work is laziness. Will with work is purpose pursuant to an ever improving reality.

No matter how far we advance technology, it'll never be as good as the real thing. So it is that amongst the greatest ironies of human history will be that, at the end of technological advancement, after all the arrogant presumption over becoming ever more superior, such a great animal that we're greater than the divinity that most scientists dismiss, we'll realize that natural existence is the pinnacle of existence. Science will eventually prove the existence of the unitive force of being, aka God, or Spirit, and will discover that everything it's created and believed to be superior to nature is but a poor facsimile of it. "We shall not cease from exploration, and the end of all our exploring will be to arrive where we started and know the place for the first time." We'll finally value everything that we take for granted when we find that the natural existential construct was always superior to everything created to supersede it, and the

God that we thought we were supplanting can't be beaten, and that we've always been exploring It, and creating reality from It.

The point of spacetime, energy and matter is to grant infinity to One, such that the timeless, singular Source may experience Itself, Us, as the perfectly perpetual plurality. Matter literally only *matters* as a vehicle for the everlasting energy, as forms of the formlessness painted across the existential canvas of spacetime. The experience of that existence is the point, the innate meaning and purpose of the existential construct. What grants purpose to every point painted across the canvas is that it's painted by the Self-perpetuating, shapeless Source through an endless succession of shapes, or 'selves.'

We're selves of the selfless, all-selves-encompassing-Self. So it is that the Great Mystery is the unending eternity of the Self experienced as the forever finalizing, reformulating existence of infinite selves, the One painting the infinite upon One canvas.

Religion is the error of defining the Undefinable as something specific, usually based upon the motive of selling something specific in order to control the buyer. Spirituality is the experiencing of and thinking about the Undefinable, without the motive compelling the mistake of making it anything specific, for it's within everything and, therefore, any attempt to say it's any specific part of that thing is making the mistake of saying it's not equally within every other part of that thing. What you call it and how you symbolize it are as the finite of Its infinity.

The boastful always dupe the simpleminded, because they can't grasp the substance with their minds, they can only grasp the show. Thus are the simpleminded enslaved by whoever puts on the best show, whereas the wise know that the show is typically performed to conceal the lack of substance.

Poverty is measured in money and possession. Wealth is measured in love and purpose.

The value of anything is in its utility to life. The enslavement of anything is in the illusion of it being ownable by life.

What separates the scientist and the mystic is that the scientist is trained to focus on and accentuate the distinctions, whilst the mystic is left untrained (or prompted to forget conventional training) so as to sense and focus on the indistinction. One makes measures of and manipulates the measurable, classifying and enforcing a falsely absolute separation, the other senses and ascribes language to the immeasurable, connecting towards total connection and reducing to the point of irreducibility. The physics win the impermanent physical contest, typically for the sake of the greed and the pride of the ego, the metaphysics wins the permanent spiritual contest, typically for the sake of peace and personal emancipation from the ego's artificially imposed confines and greedy pursuits.

There was no beginning. There won't be an end. It's a truth that the finite form can't fully grasp, but that's forever held by that which, or whom, every form is borrowed by Itself.

The essential nature of humanity is to be one with God, with nature, and with one another. When aware of and operating based upon this essential unification, humanity is unconquerable. This is why the base strategic evil of divide, disempower and conquer is to: (1) divide humankind from itself, turning its innate brotherhood into cutthroat competition and tribal warfare of one kind or another, and (2) divide humankind from its innate divinity and inseparability from God through religion and its teaching of a false separation from God and those of other religions, and (3) divide humankind from the natural world, teaching of Mother Nature not as the Holy Mother, but, instead, as having no Spirit or consciousness and simply being a collection of land and dead resources to be plundered and controlled. So long as humankind remains deceived by these manufactured delusions of division, and owned by this old divide and conquer strategy, divided in its collective mind from itself through various tribalistic identities, divided from its divinity and divided from its roots intertwined with those of Mother Nature, all of which are actually inseparable and can only be separated in mind, we're enslaved. Salvation will come from tearing down these boundaries of the dividers and conquerors. Freedom will come with the collective-Self-discovery of a spiritual unity revealing that we belong to one another, to the Holy Mother, and to the eternal One.

To those deceived by the lies by which the status quo is conserved, all legitimate truth is controversial, and all false truth is packaged and sold as acceptable. Anything outside the box is offensive, propriety setting the seams.

Seers can't show you the truth directly, but can point you in the right direction. Every revelation is made by glimpsing the truth directly, with the right words being like signposts pointing you towards such sights.

The truth is agonizing in its acquisition; most simply can't withstand the suffering required to reach it, and pain themselves with the desperate gripping onto the ungraspable.

Abstaining from what makes you weaker makes you stronger. Doing what makes you stronger makes you stronger still. These are the dual self-honoring disciplines without which best self and best life shall elude us.

The average critic doesn't consider the creator, they only consider themselves. Like the average person's experience of the world in general, the outer world becomes a self-reflecting self-projection. Criticism in general is less about the quality of the work and more about the attempt to stuff it into a box of the critic's expectation and preconception. If three-fifths of the creation fits into the box, the creation receives three out of five stars.

If you think tribally in terms like "my people," you're immediately creating a separation between those of a certain ethnicity or group and everyone else, making you a part of the division and conflict that undermines all collaboration, unity and shared spiritual identity that creates all peace and progress. Justice in both thought and action is always universal in its consideration and application.

The purpose of suffering is to prevent future suffering. Symptoms are signals of the need for a cure.

Following one's dreams, one's heart, one's central truth, is the foremost struggle of every life. At some point everyone gets in touch with their innermost Self, the eternal spiritual aspect around which the biological form is formed; their little God. And the little God tells them what to do. And they instantly know that they should do it, because it's a directive of their truest Self. But when they go outside of that Self into the world to make their dreams true, the world almost always tells them: "No!" "No, you can't do that; you can't be that. You have to be *this*. You can't be the Self, that doesn't fit. You have to be a self to fit this way into society, as expected by society." And this sets the battleground for every life: Can you hear as many no's as will be required, and respond "Yes!" within your deepest, truest Self, and keep moving towards Self-realization regardless of how many no's you hear until they turn into "Yes?" That's the one test: Do you believe enough in your truest, deepest Self, and Its dreams for you and your Self-realization, to fight through the No's until the negations are overcome and turn into Self-affirmations? Do you have the belief, the faith, required to be who you truly are, or will you fail the test of faith and capitulate to societal conquering?

The truth is always felt, never known. What is known is the shadow cast by the truth, not the truth itself. The heart senses the truth, the mind only imitates it. The holy light shines through Its infinitely-faceted Self, the truth of It seen relative to the clarity of self.

Success is simply a matter of bringing the mind into alignment with the heart while supporting and strengthening the body that hosts the complete alignment. And yet, despite this simplicity, few achieve success, for simplification of complexity is difficult.

Fuck being borne along by mere survival. If you have no love, no passion for what you're doing, you shouldn't be doing it. Better to retreat to subsist in the forest as long as you can than to live in service to loveless wealth.

The unrecognized cost: You reduce yourself by reducing 'others,' because, at the base of being, there are no others. Otherness is an illusion that only your heart can see through.

***

The best sex happens when the body becomes an extension of the heart.

***

Practice breathing.

***

The path leads in, not out. Wherever you go out into the world, you're projecting your inner state upon it. The extrinsic is a mirror of the immanent. Peaceful environments help keep the peace within, but can't supplant it. When you're annoyed, stressed, not at peace within, that's what you'll find in your environment, even on the serenest mountaintop. Go in. Sink into the ceaseless Self. Sitting in the holy within, so shall the outer be.

The truth is a moving target, except for the One truth. All other truth is subject to the orientation of the subject and its objects.

I don't agree with the foundational capitalistic premise that I have to pay someone for the right to be alive. I don't believe that I should have to either pay someone or else take advantage of others so that they pay the bill for me. The entire construct is a 'bill of goods.' No bill should be due. THAT'S what's unsustainable about it. It's inherently unsustainably parasitic, forcing the planet and humanity to play the sick host. It's also against our symbiotic, mutualistic nature as humans. And THAT'S why so many have the urge to retreat from the enslaving system into the woods, where drawing breath is free of charge. THAT'S why the progressive seekers will ALWAYS reject it on a bodily level, and be compelled to form mutualistic, sustainable 'communes' outside its clenches. Let me cleanse myself of all unclean and unnatural impositions invented to control and feed off of me and my brethren, and be my true, free, natural self.

Those that're loved are those that love themselves. Like everything else, the outer world is a reflection of the inner world. When one loves oneself, it's like a natural gravitational pull for the love in the world. It sounds cliché, but it's true: finding love from another isn't about creating or discovering it, but about self-love attracting their mirroring.

There's a natural current flowing out from every heart. Our only job is to find it and ride it, as it will carry you to your shore, the place of love and purpose where you best belong.

The prevailing modern materialist paradigm of existence teaches you that fulfillment is found on the outside. If you have the right possessions, the right home, the right car, the right people around you, you'll be complete. But no one ever completes themselves this way. In truth, everyone who believes some version of this lie can only ever remain unsatisfied, because they forever seek it outside themselves, where it can't be found. This is by design, because unsatisfied people will continue producing and buying for the profiteering benefit of their economic masters, and will never feel complete. Why? Because the materialist philosophy is wrong. Ironically, chasing matter is an empty exercise in self-defeating delusion, because only the energy at the heart of the matter is real and lasting, the material forms it takes are fleeting. This is why the completion is always within, at the essence of the thing, not in the naming or control or illusive possession of the thing. Consciousness isn't an accident of a randomly mechanistic universe, but the very source of all existence. Trying to make happiness outside yourself is thereby being the duped, victimized fool. The complete self isn't something to be built from the outside, but something to be discovered on the inside. It's always been there, waiting for you to travel all the way in and sit in the center of yourself, the holy throne. Thus is the only personal salvation found the same way that economic and political and social and spiritual liberation is found: not in desperate outer seeking and accumulation of matter, but at the innermost point of your immaterial being. That which, or whom, is outside yourself that you believe makes you happy does so by leading you inside yourself, for the essence of everything that you believe is without is the same as what's within.

Pretentious philosophy complicates with technicality. True philosophy distills into simplicity. Poor philosophy adds, whereas sagacity is purification towards essence. It's easy to add the unnecessary. It's difficult to remove everything occluding the necessity.

Matter is heavy. It feels the burden of its own weight, especially when it's sickened, embodied matter. When it's well, it feels no such burden. Energy, on the other hand, has no weight. Mind may be either. It may be the pure energy of Consciousness, of Self, or it may carry the weight of the world and the self. Like light being wave or particle, mind chooses its nature at every moment. By its focused concern or unfocused lack of concern it may carry the weight of the world by focusing on the forever insecure ego and its past slights and its future hopes and fears, or it may drop this weight and float in the weightless center, where it's everything and nothing at once. It may be unfixed, pure potential, or fixed and finite. Every mind chooses every moment: weight or weightlessness. Wave or particle. Self or self.

Spacetime and matter exist so that all being may exist and everything may be experienced by every form of existence. It's an existential construct that exists for the innate and inherent value of existence. It's all a means for the One thing to exist as and experience everything, all for the sake of Itself.

Money is just a hidden mode of slavery. The more present and forceful of a focus it is in your life, the more enslaved you are. It should be passed on to aid and improve life, else turn you into its obedient subject. And the same may be said of any power we attain through others, and our egotistic ideas of ourselves. If it serves life it's worthy. If it subjugates life, it sickens and enslaves. True life, true freedom, is subject only to itself; to the service of itself; to the service of life in its totality; in its perfect inclusivity. If serving one person, family or tribal identity over any other, it can only be unjust, as with the ego, as with all money hoarded unapplied to life.

What you feel matters exponentially more than what you think. The feeling is the source sound, the thought is but the echo.

Everything said to be 'new' or 'created' is but a reformation of what existed before it, going all the way back to a 'beginning' that has always been, and, thus, never truly began. So it is that physics' "nothing is created or destroyed, only forever rearranged" is the same as the spiritual truth that all things are One Thing, the eternal energy 'big banged' into the source energy condensed and materialized into Infinite of One. This is the nature of an existence that has always been and always will be: deathlessness experienced through death; formlessness experienced through form; infinity experienced through the finite.

The people of the West know very little of true spirituality, only its disempowering, antithetical pretense. Christianity, the prevalent western religion, teaches that God is separate from and above a nature that's inherently sinful. The truth is that nature is an embodiment of God, and that all of its forms are manifestations of the formless Source. Christianity teaches an egotistic, idolatrous obsession with one prophet, when, again, divinity is ubiquitous, and everyone has a prophet in their hearts. Christianity teaches a tribalistic separatist identity, and of a soul separate from others, and a religious supremacy, when the true spiritual identity is universal, there's only one soul, Spirit, shared equally by all, and no one religion can ever be supreme, as all religion contains some truth while teaching versions of these falsehoods. And it's not an accident that Christianity, as an extension of imperial history, teaches these inherently divisive, disempowering lies. As part of a conservatism that conserves the wealth and power of the few at the cost of the many, Christianity is the spiritual deception that's a part of the greater conservative deceptive strategy governing all of its social theory: Divide and Conquer. Whereas truth is always of an empowering, opposing nature: Unite and Liberate.

Nature is just the evolution of material condensations of Spirit relative to spacetime.

The modern world is ruled by the four P's: political correctness, propaganda, profiteering and pride (or ego). It's as fake, artificial and unnatural as plastic. Most of the world is plastic-wrapped, whereas all true spirituality practices removing the wrapping.

God is conscious source energy experiencing Its singular immortality through infinite mortality. Science describes the form and phenomena caused by Its expansion from One into Infinite of One. Nature is the evolution of Its material condensations relative to Its spacetime environment.

You're not an American being, you're being an American. Those who find the most authentic form of themselves in America find that they're being *in* America, not that they're an American, or even being American. Drop every way in which you're trained to act and think for the benefit of your masters, and there lies your true, untrainable Self.

Everyone's in such a big damn ego-driven hurry to get where they think they need to be and become who they think they need to become that no one is ever where or who they are. No place is more important than wherever you are. No version of you is truer than the undefined version. So there's such a cruel irony in the fact that the modern world drives us to become a 'successful person'

when the greatest success is finding the unchanging version of your core self that was concealed by all the outward searching. It's a self that's entirely unchanged by possession and egotistic accoutrements of 'success.' And the more you surround yourself with these illusions of self and accessories of success, the more you occlude your truest self. The irony deepens when we find that the 'land of the free and home of the brave' is the land of those enslaved to egotistic and covetous pursuits that few are brave enough to free themselves of. So it is that enslavement is an outward accentuation of false needs that you need not have, whereas freedom is an inward discovery of what you've been all along.

Enlightenment is to see existence as the flesh of the Self, of which one's own flesh is an indivisible part.

Love is the echo of the infinite; the endlessness resounding within the chamber of being.

We're naturally divine beings bastardizing divinity and making ourselves ever more unnatural for the sake of finally knowing, appreciating and returning to both things, which are essentially the same thing.

The Lord's Prayer, Redux:

Maketh me what You will.

I know nothing without my heart. My mind just picks up on and translates the reverberation echoing within my vessel. It's always the heart that strikes the gong.

When you begin to dig at the root, you begin to sense everything to be a sign or a signal.

Money is the poor man's wealth.

The only thing beyond doubt is love, and yet no one can define it, materialism disproven.

God is infinity founding the finite, immortality made into mortality, the formless endlessly reformed, ubiquity ever uniquely unfurling.

***

Imprisonment is incomplete until the prisoner believes that he/she is free.

What is meditation, and why do sages link it to the concept of enlightenment? A thinking mind is bound by its thoughts, whereas a mind without conception sits in the pure perception of what unpretentiously is. A mind clinging to a limited conception of what is cannot possess the full truth, only a fraction of it, whilst its ego convinces it of a possession that has slipped through its fingers. It holds but a measly fraction of what fully is whilst its ego tells it that it holds what is, like cupping one's hands to the river and coming up with the belief that the river is held. The mind is thereby misled relative to its ideas, whether about itself, others, or the world. For oneself, others, and the world are simply too complex and too causally interdependent to be perfectly comprehended in isolation. As Oscar Wilde said: "To define is to limit." And so how can anything be perfectly defined, and how can anything or anyone be truly known in thought? For all idea, all grasping for truth, is without the ability to reflect the entire truth, for every idea lacks some measure of information, and every mind, like every computer, lacks some measure of capacity in translating that incomplete data into perfect truth. Whereas to simply observe the truth of things without conception is to experience them directly, without artificial constraint. So it is that truth is perfect observation without conception, and ignorance is conception without perfect observation. Thus are we always in some state of ignorance while we're thinking, and are we only experiencing truth when we free ourselves from thought, in the purest possible state of observation.

We're all students. We're all teachers. Every teacher that doesn't learn from his/her students, and realize that not just everyone but everything has something to teach him/her, is yet to become the true teacher. Like everything else, education is reciprocal.

If you're aware of the injustices and do nothing to address them, then you're complicit in and silently condoning them. This is why most people make sure to be as unaware of as much of the world's evils as they can, trading complicity for ignorance.

Ego is insecurity. Everything it does is to grow, confirm and defend itself. Anything that threatens that idea of self shakes the security of that self. The only security comes when you're not aware of yourself, and are thus closer to the divine non-self. Every target can be struck except the one that doesn't exist.

To be pure of faith is to practice radical acceptance. The pure faith of radical acceptance is to have a sense of source Self and to know that, by the preeminent law of causality, everything originated in Source, the First Cause, such that there's a divinely sourced cascading cause for everything that succeeded it, continuing forever. Everything that happens and everything that exists is thereby an inevitable effect of the First

Cause; the cause of the One big banging into Infinite of One. Radical acceptance says that everything that has happened and will happen does so out of causal necessity. It doesn't mean everything that you THINK could happen will happen, and that you need to accept every thought and idea had by yourself and others, it simply says that occurrence is an effect of necessity. It means that every actor is enacting everything that formed him/her/it, and could do no other than act accordingly, as every action is a reaction to every preceding action. It doesn't mean you relinquish your free will, it means you freely will your fate along with everything and everyone else. When you embrace this faith, this Amor Fati, when you fully understand and believe it, you let go of the pains of the past and don't worry about the possible pains of the future, because you've accepted that it's all necessary; you're not qualifying it as good or bad, just needed.

Even absent a belief in God, by understanding that causality is complete you may have faith.

All roads lead to the truth, typically through doubt and dishonesty. Because even as we doubt ourselves and lie to ourselves on behalf of our egos, the truth is the only thing that survives. As all illusion and lie inexorably fades into oblivion, the truth forever remains the only inextinguishable thing; an endlessly enduring echo of the Source. So even as some circle it, drawing ever nearer while never quite reaching it, and some follow their egos and drive as fast as they can away from it, not realizing that existence is as the infinite snake eating its own tail, all must inevitably crash, fall into or otherwise return to it. Akin to death, it may come like a road wreck, reality forcing itself upon denial, or like an epiphany, for it's the terminus of the inroad.

Truth and reality run relative to the universality of their application. If it's true of and for everyone and everything, it's absolutely true. If it's true only for one person it's akin to illusion or delusion for/to everyone and everything else. Most of our ideas about ourselves fall near to the latter; we turn our self-delusions into illusive reality by our belief in them, projecting our imagined self upon our reality. The more that we believe what we imagine of ourselves, the more that we make it true relative to ourselves, the more we may convince others of this delusion relative to the confidence of our projection.

One cannot find The Way without having first gone astray. There's no knowing the right path except by knowing its differentiation from the wrong path. Thus are sages made by evil, is sagacity bred by suffering, and is light visible relative to the darkness.

Existence isn't as meaningful as you make it, it's as meaningful as you *allow it to be*. Existence, and the life that springs from it, is inherently meaningful, and constitutes its own point. You may strive for what you want, and finding and growing love will enrich your life, but you can't make your life any more meaningful than it innately is, and love is absorbable everywhere to those attuned to it. Thus is the meaning of life made most available to those whom absorb it by completely noticing and embracing it. Life is the only point for lifeforms, as existence is all there is. When you accept it unequivocally, without qualification, you remain open to this inherent meaning, and are thereby able to see and absorb more of the inherent meaning and value of the present moments constituting life. But, instead, we qualify and judge and separate ourselves from it. The more that we do this, the more that our beliefs and attitudes and mental distraction narrows our perceptions, the more that we're outside the present in our egos and our belief in anything that pulls us away from the present (such as by focusing on an afterlife or the idea in a reincarnating soul or by imposing upon our perception and acceptance of reality that some things are absolutely good and others are absolutely bad, rather than that all things are necessary, interdependent and inseparable from existence), the more that we close ourselves off from absorbing life's innate worth and thereby reduce the meaning manifest in every moment.

Trust should never extend past mutual benefit. And the only way to prevent a future uprising is justice. Therefore, the only way for there to be enduring social trust and collaboration is for everyone to benefit relative to merit, the basis of social idealism.

Genius is the super-sanity of recognizing the common insanity, for which the genius is awarded by being labeled insane.

The purpose of the symptom is to show you that something is wrong. You place your hand on a hot stove, the symptom is the feeling of your burning flesh. Conventional western medicine responds by numbing your hand so that you don't feel the symptom and ignore the cause, allowing them to sell you concealment of the symptom for life, dissuading you from finding and treating the cause. This keeps you weak and dependent upon patronizing their chemical salesmen. The more symptoms to conceal, the greater the western medicinal success, because success is based upon profitability; upon keeping you chained in mind and body to their profiteers. True medicine pulls your hand away, success achieved when patronizing the healer is no longer required.

To 'meditate' is to observe something without thinking about it; without reducing it with words, ideas and definitions, without projecting your ego or preconceived, limiting notions upon it, and thereby to see it truly, in its pure, undefinable aspect; to see it in the manner reflecting Oscar Wilde's: "To define is to limit." Only by seeing the undefinable thing are you seeing that thing truly, without artificial limit, including yourself. As soon as you begin applying language and egotistic definitions to it in reflection of the self that you believe that you are, you're only able to see a fraction of that thing, or that artificial aspect of that thing that reflects your egotistic self. So it is that to meditate is to observe as the spiritual Self that isn't applying the artifices of the egotistic self.

Everything is my Self.

Mushrooms help to relatively unfix consciousness. Less fixed to the bounded self, you're freer to explore and experience the boundless Self.

Money is enslavement. You're either enslaved to it as a freeing, ego-accentuating force (if you have an abundance of it), or you're enslaved to it as a limiting, ego-reducing force (if you have a scarcity of it), the latter enslavement feeding the former. The secret is that it's not actually *required* for life, which is why the only liberation is offered by self-sustaining properties and communities, regardless of their labeling.

Where do you think the *income* is coming from? For all income there's something out of which it's drawn, and what do you think the eventual *outcome* will be?

The methods of divination are endless, as many as the mind is open to, as infinite possible reflections of the self peering upon its Self.

The Tao, The Way, is the way of nature. Nothing hurried, nothing forced, nothing fabricated, everything simply flowing out from and rebecoming itself, all self an evolution of the One made infinite.

Suspending time is being subsumed by Spirit.

Skepticism exists on a spectrum. Too little skepticism, too much denial of doubt, too much allowance for what's possible, and you become a mark to be conned by the unscrupulous always looking for ways to take advantage of disadvantage. Too much skepticism, too much depth of doubt, too little allowance for what's possible, and you con yourself, closing yourself off to truths that you presume are false because they don't fit your preconceptions. Ignorance and naïveté cultivate the former, science and arrogance cultivate the latter. Alas, most people understand ignorance and naïveté to be absolute negatives, when, in truth, they're largely akin to humility, for not presuming to understand everything is the removal of the blinders of false knowledge needed to understand *anything*. In the modern world the latter, more skeptical type of mindset dominates, the closed mind that only sees what it believed going into the presentation of an idea, thus missing truths it presumes false, and teaching that the cost of the scientific mindset is similar to the cost of the religious mindset: nothing is visible that wasn't visible *before* being presented. So it is that what's needed are minds open to greater possibilities, to a type of limitless potential of what's possible, to a knowledge built upon universal principles that can never belong to one religion and that may not have been confirmed yet by limiting scientific instrumentation and paradigms, only closing when impossibility has been *proven*. Thus we see that skepticism is both a necessary shield against being preyed upon by propagandists and con artists, and the lies underlying misleading, mind-closing ideologies like conservatism, materialism and realism, while also, when the shield becomes too large, becoming akin to blinders producing a type of myopia against seeing possibility. The goal is to limit, and ideally negate, the projection and mirroring effects of the ego: we project what we believe we already know about ourselves and the world onto the world as we move through and observe it, and *that's* what's reflected back to us, obscuring our observational capacity. Only when we turn the projector off do we truly see, and only by seeing possibility may we glimpse truth. So the mental discipline pursuant of truth dictates that neither should we project and use the world as our mirror, nor should we absorb the projections of others, but allow for pure observation to permit any and all possible truth until discernment disproves it.

www.ingramcontent.com/pod-product-compliance
Lightning Source LLC
Chambersburg PA
CBHW060538160125
20421CB00040B/1183